Japan Through the Lens of the Tokyo Olympics

I0129093

This book situates the 2020 Tokyo Olympics within the social, economic, and political challenges facing contemporary Japan. Using the 2020 Tokyo Olympics as a lens into the city and the country as a whole, the stellar line up of contributors offers hidden insights and new perspectives on the Games. These include city planning, cultural politics, financial issues, language use, security, education, volunteerism, and construction work. The chapters then go on to explore the many stakeholders, institutions, citizens, interest groups, and protest groups involved, and feature the struggle over Tokyo's extreme summer heat, food standards, the implementation of diversity around disabilities, sexual minorities, and technological innovations. Giving short glimpses into the new Olympic sports, this book also analyses the role of these sports in Japanese society.

Japan Through the Lens of the Tokyo Olympics will be of huge interest to anyone attending the Olympic Games in Tokyo 2020. It will also be useful to students and scholars of the Olympics and the sociology of sport, as well as Japanese culture and society.

Barbara Holthus, Ph.D., is a sociologist and deputy director of the German Institute for Japanese Studies, Tokyo, Japan. Her main research interests include marriage and the family, childcare, happiness and well-being, media, as well as demographic change. Publications include *Life Course, Happiness and Well-being in Japan* (2017, Routledge, ed. with W. Manzenreiter).

Isaac Gagné, Ph.D., a cultural anthropologist, is a senior research fellow at the German Institute for Japanese Studies, Tokyo, Japan and managing editor of *Contemporary Japan*. He works on mental health and social welfare, morality and ethics, and religion. Publications include "Religious globalization and reflexive secularization in a Japanese new religion" (2017, *Japan Review*).

Wolfram Manzenreiter is professor of Japanese Studies at the University of Vienna, Austria. His research is concerned with social and anthropological aspects of sports, emotions, rural Japan, and transnational networks of the Japanese diaspora. Publications include *Sport and Body Politics in Japan* (2014, Routledge).

Franz Waldenberger is an economist and director of the German Institute for Japanese Studies, Tokyo, Japan. His research focuses on the Japanese Economy in comparative perspective. Recent publications include "Society 5.0. Japanese ambitions and initiatives" in *The Digital Future* (2018, Konrad Adenauer Stiftung).

Japan Through the Lens of the Tokyo Olympics

Edited by
Barbara Holthus,
Isaac Gagné,
Wolfram Manzenreiter, and
Franz Waldenberger

Routledge
Taylor & Francis Group
LONDON AND NEW YORK

DIJ

First published 2020
by Routledge
2 Park Square, Milton Park, Abingdon, Oxon OX14 4RN

and by Routledge
52 Vanderbilt Avenue, New York, NY 10017

Routledge is an imprint of the Taylor & Francis Group, an informa business

British Library Cataloguing-in-Publication Data
A catalogue record for this book is available from the British Library

Library of Congress Cataloging-in-Publication Data
Names: Holthus, Barbara G., editor. | Gagné, Isaac, editor. | Manzenreiter, Wolfram, editor. | Waldenberger, Franz, 1961- editor. | Routledge (Firm)
Title: Japan through the lens of the Tokyo Olympics / edited by Barbara Holthus, Isaac Gagné, Wolfram Manzenreiter and Franz Waldenberger .
Description: First Edition. | New York : Routledge, 2020. | Includes bibliographical references and index. | Identifiers: LCCN 2019058163 (print) | LCCN 2019058164 (ebook) | ISBN 9780367469573 (Hardback) | ISBN 9780367471682 (Paperback) | ISBN 9781003033905 (eBook) | ISBN 9781000057591 (Adobe PDF) | ISBN 9781000057652 (mobi) | ISBN 9781000057713 (ePub)
Subjects: LCSH: Olympics–Planning. | Olympics–Political aspects–Japan–Tokyo. | Olympics–Economic aspects–Japan–Tokyo. | Olympics–Social aspects–Japan–Tokyo. | Olympics–Security measures–Japan–Tokyo–Planning. | Japan–Social life and customs. | Popular culture–Japan–Tokyo.
Classification: LCC GV721.5 .J36 2020 (print) | LCC GV721.5 (ebook) | DDC 796.48–dc23
LC record available at https://lccn.loc.gov/2019058163
LC ebook record available at https://lccn.loc.gov/2019058164

ISBN: 978-0-367-46957-3 (hbk)
ISBN: 978-0-367-47168-2 (pbk)
ISBN: 978-1-003-03390-5 (ebk)

Typeset in Times New Roman
by Wearset Ltd, Boldon, Tyne and Wear

"Written by leading experts on Japanese sport and society, this is the perfect guide for anyone – sports fan, tourist, or armchair viewer – wanting to know the inside story about the Games and Japan in the 21st century." Packed with information about the city, Olympic sports, and wider social issues in Japan, the book provides snapshots, in a pocket-sized form, of the essential background to the Olympics in 2020.

John Horne, *Waseda University, Japan*

"This is the first – and possibly only – book which explains contemporary Japan through the prism of the Olympics and the Olympics through the lens of Japanese society. Full of fascinating insights and information, it is sure to become a bible for anyone intending to attend (or even just watch) the 2020 Olympics in Tokyo. Definitely a winner."

Roger Goodman, *University of Oxford, UK*

"There is much more on the line at the 2020 Tokyo Summer Olympics than the competition among the athletes. The impacts of the Games themselves, and their lead-up and legacy, will be equally portentous for Tokyo and for Japan. This comprehensive collection by experienced Japan researchers offers highly informative and smartly written commentaries on the social, political, and economic ramifications of Tokyo 2020. Urban infrastructure, regional disparities, food sustainability, school curriculum, political jockeying, LGBTQ rights, and language diversity are just some of the topics surveyed in these absorbing essays. This is an essential briefing for anyone wishing to know what is at stake as Tokyo hosts this global sporting mega-event."

William W. Kelly, *Yale University, USA*

"This book is the perfect companion for the 2020 Tokyo Olympics. Its short, readable chapters by Japan specialists are full of intriguing information about past and present Olympics in Tokyo, and how hosting the Olympic games reshapes the city of Tokyo. The authors are solid scholars with deep experience of living and working in Tokyo. They dig far beyond the tourist images to show us how the Olympics either help to overcome social problems or simply hide them from view. Take this book along as you ride the trains and explore the city. It will be valuable long after the last medal has been awarded."

Patricia Steinhoff, *University of Hawaii, USA*

"This volume assembles scholars with a broad spectrum of expertise who provide a thorough overview of the key topics surrounding the Tokyo 2020 Olympics. Most impressive is that it blends keen analysis of the major issues for Japan with equally keen analysis of the major issues for the Olympic Games. This insightful overview of the intersection of Japan with the Olympics has something for everyone, whether academics, journalists, fans of Olympics, or fans of Japan."

Susan Brownell, *University of Missouri-St. Louis, USA*

"This is a richly informative book by social scientists analyzing numerous facets of Japan, Tokyo, and the 2020 Tokyo Summer Olympics from multiple perspectives. The 34 chapters cover a wide range of topics – including politics, economy, society, culture, media, cinema, architecture, and, of course, sports – to provide the reader with keen insights into how, in leading up to 2020, Japan is shaping, and being shaped, by the Olympics. An outstanding guide for those seeking to understand contemporary Japan and its future direction."

Glen S. Fukushima, *Former President, American Chamber of Commerce, Japan*

Contents

Figures

Contributors

Peter Backhaus, Waseda University, Tokyo.

Isaac Gagné, DIJ, Tokyo.

Sonja Ganseforth, DIJ, Tokyo.

Steffen Heinrich, Free University Berlin.

Katharina Heyer, University of Hawai'i at Manoa.

Maki Hirayama, Meiji University, Tokyo.

Barbara Holthus, DIJ, Tokyo.

Hanno Jentzsch, DIJ, Tokyo.

Axel Klein University of Duisburg-Essen.

Nora Kottmann, DIJ, Tokyo.

Daniel Kremers, DIJ, Tokyo.

Jan Lukas Kuhn, University of Trier.

Ralph Lützeler, University of Vienna.

Wolfram Manzenreiter, University of Vienna.

Sebastian Polak-Rottmann, University of Vienna.

Florian Purkarthofer, University of Vienna.

Franz Waldenberger, DIJ, Tokyo.

Torsten Weber, DIJ, Tokyo.

Preface

When Barbara first put the idea about this edited volume to paper it was April 2018. At that point, it was more than two years ahead of the Olympic Games and four years after Japan won the bid to host the Games on September 7, 2013. Tokyo had been visibly gearing up for this mega-event for a long time, as it has a history of prior unsuccessful bids for Olympic Games, the most recent for the 2016 Summer Games. Just before leaving for her second assignment at the German Institute for Japanese Studies (DIJ), Barbara typed the concept into her laptop in her former children's room at her dad's house in Hamburg. She pitched it to the DIJ team in May, our editorial team was quickly formed, and everyone jumped onto writing their chapters. Even though it found an immediate positive response from all sides, none of us could have envisioned that 17 months later, we would already have finalized our book manuscript. Exactly a year before the Tokyo 2020 Games and in the midst of the "1 Year to Go!" campaign, the editorial team met for our own several-week-long marathon editing session, suffering through Japan's scorching heat to finish the full draft. We have come this far thanks to the amazing collegiality, cooperation, and most of all the scholarship and passion of our authors.

Anyone who lives in or has visited Tokyo in the past few years will know that the Olympics are everywhere in the city. One of the key players in organizing and promoting the Olympics is the Tokyo Metropolitan Government, which has its striking building in the middle of Shinjuku and hosts numerous events to spark excitement about the Olympics for its citizens and foreigners alike (see Figure 0.1).

Among those are the exhibit of the Olympic medals, but also a photo-op area, where city government staff are readily available to take visitors' photos next to Olympic flags, in front of a racetrack photo wall, holding the Olympic torch, or together with the Olympic mascots. In addition, Figure 0.2 below shows the countdown to the Olympics and Paralympics. These markers of time are scattered throughout the city, such as inside

Figure 0.1 Tokyo Metropolitan Government building.
Source: © Wolfram Manzenreiter.

stores, at the airport, in public buildings, or at the tourist offices in major tourist destinations. Ignoring the Olympics is not an option! The same goes for our many friends who work in businesses and universities throughout the city. They tell us how their employers debate, and debate, and debate about what they should do during the Olympics, such as potentially offering telework to their employees (something extraordinarily rare in Japan), or moving final university exams to avoid potential disruption and to free students from their study obligations to be available for Olympic volunteer work – heavily criticized by some, who compare it to Japan's wartime mobilization of its youth. Mobilization or not, the city and its residents are inextricably tied up with the Olympic project, just as we have become in writing this book.

Many have aided in this project coming to life. Besides huge thanks to our families, who had to take the backseat every so often when the writing or editing kept us much longer at our desks than anticipated, we thank, first and foremost, the authors for their fantastic scholarship that we were allowed to accumulate within these pages. We further thank Jan Lukas

Figure 0.2 The editorial team, Tokyo Metropolitan Government building, 2019.
Source: © Barbara Holthus.

Kuhn for his help with the Twitter campaign for the book (we can be found at @dij_Tokyo2020 where we tweet daily about interesting facts surrounding the Olympics – follow us!); Tiffany Pitsch for her work in image editing and Claus Harmer for the cover image; and Stephanie Rogers and Georgina Bishop for indulging us in our endeavor to have this book bridge general and academic publishing, something rather uncommon in our academic environment. We sincerely hope the book will be a pleasant read and provide an interesting and informative window onto Japan as a whole, not just the mega-event itself.

Barbara, Franz, Isaac, and Wolfram
Tokyo, Fall 2019

Note on currencies and name order: Throughout the book we converted yen amounts to dollars with a conversion rate of 100 yen to a dollar. Japanese names are written in the way officially decided by the Japanese government for the romanization of names, namely last name followed by first name.

Postscript
The New Olympic Race against COVID-19

In late December 2019, China reported the discovery of a disease caused by a novel coronavirus, dubbed COVID-19. By March 12, 2020, cases worldwide exceeded 130,000, many countries went into lockdown, and speculations about cancellation or delay of the Olympics grew rampant. Yet that day, the Olympic flame lighting ceremony took place in Olympia, Greece, and the IOC and the Japanese government seemed to be out of sync with the rest of the world. Then on March 24, exactly 4 months before the Games were scheduled to start, Prime Minister Abe announced that Tokyo 2020 would be postponed to "no later than Summer 2021." For the second time in Japan's history, the Tokyo Olympics would not take place as planned, also marking the first time in Olympic history that the Games are delayed.

This book, entering the world at a time of global uncertainty, captures the buildup to Tokyo 2020 and the changes that this mega-event already produced in the economic, political, and social fabric of life, irrespective of whether the Games are held in 2020 or 2021. At the time of writing this postscript, five days after the decision for postponement and just as we are going into print, the IOC and the Japanese government seem intent on maintaining the name "Tokyo 2020." The economic distress of the postponement, as dire as it will be, will nonetheless pale in comparison to the economic impact of the pandemic. Yet, a multitude of unknowns remain. How to renegotiate corporate sponsorships for another year? What to do with the Athlete's Village condominiums, which have already been sold to new tenants expecting to move in by Fall 2020? How to maintain the 110,000 Olympic volunteers?

With millions of moving parts involved, the most unpredictable aspect is the virus itself. Will Tokyo 2020 outrun COVID-19? The race against the virus may be one of the most important challenges facing modern society. Experts say that societies—Japan included—need to prepare for both a short sprint of mitigation and a marathon of long-term containment lasting 12 to 18 months or more. If Japan—and the world—can truly pull off successful control of the virus, and if Tokyo 2020 in 2021 does in fact take place, the characterization of Tokyo 2020 as the "Recovery Olympics" will take on a whole new meaning for the entire world. A new chapter in the history of Tokyo, Japan, the Olympics, and the world is currently unfolding, but the ending remains unwritten.

The Editors
March 2020

1 Understanding Japan through the lens of Tokyo 2020

Barbara Holthus, Isaac Gagné,
Wolfram Manzenreiter, Franz Waldenberger

The Games

The average Olympic 100-meter dash finals are over in under ten seconds. The average Olympics and Paralympics last for a combined total of 34 days of events. The Olympiad – the period from one Summer Games to the next – lasts four years. And yet preparations in the hope of becoming a host city take many more years. In the case of Tokyo 2020, they have been ongoing for over 15 years, and the legacies after the Games – in the Tokyo cityscape, the nation's economy and the national memory – will last more than a lifetime.

For the brief span of July 24 to August 8 and from August 25 to September 6, 2020, Tokyo becomes the center of global attention, and all eyes are on what records will be broken and the new heights that the athletes from around the world will reach. Whatever new Olympic and Paralympic records might be set during the Games themselves, Tokyo 2020, as it is often called in Japan, has already been record-breaking in many ways. It will feature the most Olympic events ever spread across the widest geographical area, 33 different sports and disciplines with 339 events held in 42 venues up to 1,300 kilometers apart.

Furthermore, Tokyo 2020 has the largest projected costs in the history of the Olympics, at one point estimated at nearly $30 billion, and later scaled down to $13.5 billion. At the same time, Tokyo 2020 also secured the most sponsor-driven revenue in the history of the Olympics, with over $3.7 billion secured in corporate sponsorships by June 2019. Tokyo 2020 writes also a new chapter in Olympic and Paralympic history for Japan, as well as for Asia. For Tokyo this will be the second time in 56 years to host the Summer Games, following the 1964 Tokyo Olympics – though in fact, this is technically the third time that Tokyo has been selected as host city, including the forfeited 1940 Tokyo "Phantom Olympics" that never came to be. Tokyo 2020 is thus the fifth time that an Asian city has been selected to host the Summer Games, and the fourth time that they are held in Asia, after Tokyo 1964, Seoul 1988, and Beijing 2008.

Whereas the 1964 Tokyo Olympics symbolized Japan's recovery from World War II, Tokyo 2020 is described as an opportunity to symbolize Japan's recovery from the so-called two lost decades of the 1990s–2000s and the massive devastation of the March 11, 2011 earthquake, tsunami, and nuclear meltdown in northeastern Japan. But more than simply displaying the nation's recovery – which itself has been questioned by many – Tokyo 2020 is also seen as a moment for reflecting and reimagining the nation.

After soul-searching about the place of Japan in the world amidst the political and economic rise of other nations in East Asia since the 1990s and the country's own economic stagnation, including losing its place as the number two economy in the world to China, the Japanese government has been looking for opportunities to show how Japan is still an important player in the world. The 2020 Tokyo Olympics and Paralympics are an opportunity for Japan to showcase its international standing and contribution, its cultural values and technological advancement, as well as its sporting prowess. Tokyo 2020 is constructed as an important moment of redefinition for the nation vis-à-vis the global community, as well as *to itself* and its people.

The city

Like the Olympics themselves, Japan's capital has displayed hyperbolic growth since 1964. Greater Tokyo, which includes the neighboring prefectures of Saitama, Chiba, and Kanagawa, is by far the biggest urban area on the planet with more than 35 million people. Tokyo proper, consisting of 23 inner wards and satellite cities in the West, had already bypassed New York as the world's largest city by 1955. Up to 2020, Tokyo's population has grown by 30% to more than 13 million inhabitants, securing Tokyo a top rank among the world's mega-cities. Tokyo occupies less than 1% of Japan's total landmass, yet in 2020 is home to more than 10% of Japan's entire population and produces about 20% of its gross domestic product (GDP).

The demand for space of an ever-growing city has left its marks on the cityscape. All the islands in Tokyo Bay, as well as large parts of the seaside, are man-made reclamation projects, mostly by waste materials, sand from dredging, soil removed from construction sites and recently also by rubble from the disaster-stricken area in Tohoku. About two million tons of landfill were being dumped each year into the bay around the time of Tokyo 1964. The growth of annual disposal peaked in 1979, and has since fallen to levels well below 1964, thanks to waste reduction and recycling programs.

In marked contrast to 1964, Tokyo in 2020 is one of the world's tallest cities, with more than 150 buildings exceeding a height of 150 meters. Within these multi-functional skyscrapers, 32% of the space is used for luxury residences. At the time of Tokyo 1964, the New Otani Hotel was the tallest building in the city with its 17 floors reaching 72 meters; by no means a skyscraper but even today a landmark in the cityscape. Bubbling real estate prices in the 1980s induced a great number of high-rise building projects. At the peak of the bubble, real estate prices for Tokyo's central Chiyoda Ward, covering less than 12km², surpassed the entire real estate value of Canada. Yet ironically the building boom took off only after the bubble burst. Nowadays the metropolitan area has thousands of buildings towering above the height of the old New Otani Hotel.

Tokyo managed to cope well with the challenges of rapid growth, once it started to tackle environmental issues that made life in the city difficult to bear following the 1964 Olympics. Nowadays, the world's biggest urban conglomeration has less air pollution, traffic jams, litter, and noise than any other mega-city. Tokyo citizens enjoy a safe environment, lots of green space, and the world's largest rail network of more than 150 lines, transporting 40 million passengers day by day. The Michelin Guide awarded the city's gourmet eateries the highest number of stars, heralding it as the world's culinary capital. In recent years Tokyo reinvented itself as the global Capital of Cool, with Harajuku, Shibuya, and Akihabara attracting Japanese popular culture fans and millions of other visitors from abroad.

The downside of Tokyo's success story is the widening gap with the rest of the country. Many in the regional peripheries are weary of decades of unipolarization and feel left behind by the steady promotion of the metropolitan area. It is here where criticism of Tokyo hosting the Olympics in 2020 was most pronounced. This criticism, together with the questioning of a pollution-free Tokyo or Japan when considering the problems of radioactivity due to the Fukushima Daiichi nuclear power plant meltdown, are however seldom visible in mainstream public discourse.

The nation

Widening regional disparities are not the only issue that Japan is confronted with. Back in the 1960s, the economic miracle was still unfolding with growth of real GDP at annual rates of 10% and higher, which was supported by a young and rapidly growing population. Entering the 1990s, annual growth declined to about 1%, accompanied by a rapidly aging and – since 2010 – even shrinking population. Government debt has risen to record-high levels, although without reliance on foreign money; in comparison, close to 30% of US national debt is owned by foreign entities.

Quite to the contrary, Japan remains the world's richest country in terms of net foreign assets. But the distribution of wealth and income has become increasingly uneven.

With income inequality and poverty rates above the OECD average, the image of a homogeneous middle-class society has vanished – even as citizens continue to see themselves as predominantly "in the middle" in terms of their own standards of living. Structural barriers continue to prevent the full integration of women and elderly workers into the labor market, which has seen a steady rise of non-regular employment. The government is well aware that to cope with the demographic challenge of low fertility, efforts need to be directed towards improving career opportunities of women, deepening international integration, and increasing productivity.

The fourfold increase in foreign tourists over the last seven years, mainly from China and Southeast Asia, is certainly impressive. The number of foreign workers, too, doubled over the last five years, although the 2% share in total employment remains very low in international comparison. The same can be said of direct investment by foreign companies in Japan. Its level of 4% relative to GDP amounts to just one tenth of the OECD average of 40%. Labor productivity has been more or less stagnant over the last 25 years and has fallen below the OECD average. This is surprising, because Japan spends more than most other OECD countries on research and development. The country has also one of the best-educated workforces. However, it seems not to be able to employ these excellent resources effectively. As a consequence, the government has been calling for a "workstyle" reform and it is betting on the digital transformation. Its framework of "Society 5.0" envisages a super-smart and fully inclusive society, where the cyber and the physical world are hoped to be "seamlessly integrated." Digitalization and connectivity are not only envisioned to close Japan's productivity gap, they are also expected to provide direct solutions in areas like disaster prevention and resilience, elderly care, regional revitalization, and climate change mitigation. But technology alone will not bring about the changes needed to secure welfare and sustainability. Leadership and entrepreneurship are indispensable when it comes to exploiting technological potentials and driving social and economic change. Fostering leadership and entrepreneurship is probably the most important, but also most difficult challenge Japan confronts.

The book

In this book, we situate the 2020 Tokyo Olympics within the social, economic, regional, political, and global changes of and challenges for Japan. The Olympics serve as a catalyst for important issues in contemporary

Japanese society, and therefore, using the 2020 Tokyo Olympics as a lens onto the city and country is our ultimate goal. We aim to explain why Japan deals with the implementation of this mega-event the way it does. These Olympics are constructed as something that as its legacy is supposed to "only bring good" to the country: embrace diversity and inclusiveness in society, foster sustainability, boost Japan's economy, be a beacon of light to improve social cohesion, create a feeling of unity and of pride for the country, increase the willingness of its citizens to volunteer for the well-being of society. Explaining how the many stakeholders, institutions, average citizens, interest groups, and protest groups deal with this and forge their own roles, counter or not, vis-à-vis this mega-event helps in understanding how Japan works, far beyond the mega-event itself. Only a publication that takes this multitude of facets into account is able to show how deeply the Olympics impact society, politics, the economy, and public discourse already for years ahead of the Games.

The editors and authors gathered in this publication are well-published Japan scholars, from the fields of political science, sociology, economics, history, anthropology, linguistics, social geography, and cultural studies. They are connected to the German Institute for Japanese Studies, DIJ for short; they are either current or former researchers of the DIJ or scholars at other universities, who are linked to the institute through other joint research projects. The DIJ is a research institute focused on contemporary Japan, and is funded by the German Federal Ministry of Education and Research. It is located in the heart of Tokyo, right across from the New Otani Hotel mentioned above, the tallest building in Tokyo in 1964. The history of the DIJ dates back to 1988, just before the beginning of the Heisei period in 1989. As we write this book in 2019, with the abdication of Emperor Akihito and the ascension of Emperor Naruhito, we entered the first year of the so-called Reiwa period. With our mission to enhance knowledge and understanding of contemporary Japan through multi- and interdisciplinary approaches, we are uniquely positioned in providing insights into the discourses and debates, changes, and events connected to bringing the Olympic Games of 2020 to Tokyo for the second time since 1964.

The book offers "hidden" insights into the Games and provides a window onto Japanese society, economics, and politics through portraying the way the Olympic Games have influenced Japanese society, government, and businesses already for years before the Games have even started. City planning and host town organization, financial issues, language use, food, security concepts, sexuality and sexual policing, school activities, volunteerism, construction work, advertising the Olympics and the Olympic sponsor system, but also the struggle over food standards, as well as the implementation of diversity in regards to disabilities, sexual minorities and partnerships are just some of the issues taken up by chapters in the book. Longer chapters are interspersed with one-page spotlights that highlight additional key issues, among them technological innovations planned to be showcased for the Olympics, the struggle with fighting Tokyo's extreme summer heat, and the Olympic mascots. We also give short glimpses of the new Olympic sports and the role of these sports in Japan.

As foreigners, non-Japanese, we have an outsider's view onto Japan and Tokyo. Yet as Japan scholars, speaking Japanese, and being long-term residents in Tokyo, we also have the privilege of an insider's perspective. This makes us especially suited for publishing this book, in more depth than foreign journalists can and with more insight than scholars who reside outside of Japan. This book is our attempt to explain Japan to those without much prior knowledge of Japan; be it university students or a generally interested audience alike. The book is illustrated with numerous images taken throughout the city to show the infiltration of the Olympics throughout the cityscape and throughout everyday urban life – be it at school entrances, in train stations, on streets, in stores, and more. Constant bombardment of Tokyo 2020-related advertising weaves through the entire fabric of social, public life.

The city and its public transport system are plastered with posters and videos in trains or on platforms for the millions of daily commuters taking one of the many lines of Tokyo Metro, one of the main local sponsors of the Olympics; numerous campaign events are held throughout the city; countdown markers can be found throughout the city in sightseeing spots, public buildings, or shops (see Figure 0.2); Olympic logos are a daily sight in the rows of products in supermarkets, displayed on sponsors' goods such as chocolate, milk, or yoghurt; TV reports help in explaining the Paralympics, the hurdles and endurance of Olympic and Paralympic hopefuls; Japanese fictional TV-series (*terebi dorama*), advertisements, museum exhibits, and anti-Olympic demonstrations (even though small) also do their part in cementing the Olympics into the consciousness and memory of those within the city, if not beyond. The building boom in the city further underlines this. The "Go Beyond 2020" campaign is one such marketing example, hinting at the legacy and sustainability of the Games for the citizens of Tokyo – an improved infrastructure, aiding diverse needs for those in wheelchairs or for parents with strollers (see Figure 1.1).

As the following pages show, the book provides a fascinating window onto Japan as a whole, not just the mega-event itself. The Olympics are so much larger than the four weeks themselves. This book is actually about *Japan 2020*, it guides through the developments and also points to

Figure 1.1 Advertising a more barrier-free Tokyo, by Tokyo Metro.
Source: © Barbara Holthus.

post-Olympics Japan and Tokyo – when the Olympic tourists have left, when hotel prices will have leveled off again, when companies can run their operations smoothly again without the significant hindrances of masses maneuvering through the city to get to the Olympic venues, when the apartments in the Olympic Village will be getting ready to be turned over to their new tenants, and when politicians and historians start reflecting on the Games, and when the actual costs will come to light. And then it is already time for Japan to start gearing for its next mega-events, such as the World Masters Games 2021, held in the Kansai region and for the first time in Asia, as well as the 2025 Osaka World Expo. Tokyo 2020 is certainly a major horizon; but as the city itself expands beyond the limits of one's vision, the future of Tokyo – and Japan – stretches far beyond the halo of the Olympic torchlight.

2   Olympics and the media

Wolfram Manzenreiter

The Olympic and Paralympic Games are the greatest media spectacle of modernity, providing a powerful platform for the host nation to communicate ideas about itself and future visions with domestic and global audiences. In terms of media reach, no other global event rivals the Games: Only the Summer Olympics have the institutional framework to bring representatives from all nation-states of the world together for the celebration of excellence, fairness, and respect under commonly agreed rules and regulations. The worldwide interest in athletics, paired with the allure of medal counts and rankings for petty nationalist ambitions, guarantee an unrivalled scope of media coverage. The IOC Marketing Report claims a global audience of 2.6 billion, or half of the worldwide TV universe, that was watching parts of the Rio 2016 Games. With over seven billion video views of official content on social media platforms, including Twitter, YouTube, and Facebook, digital media coverage exceeded conventional TV rates for the first time in history. Sales of broadcasting rights provide the IOC with multi-billion-dollar revenue streams: 74% of the IOC income of $5.6 billion for the 31st Olympiad 2013–2016 stemmed from broadcasting rights arrangements.

Television has been the most significant factor in the commercial growth of the Olympics. Satellite technology was first used for the Tokyo 1964 Olympics. The liberalization of national media systems in the 1980s lay the foundation for the Olympics business model, catering to the needs of corporations for marketing opportunities. In 2001 the IOC established OBS (Olympic Broadcasting Services) to take greater control of televising the Games. OBS produces and transmits the world feed of live coverage of every sport from every venue. Media partners can select images and events of greatest interest to their audiences. In response to the rise of internet platforms and social media services threatening to capture audiences' interest without the revenues, the IOC started the Olympic Channel in 2016 to keep up year-round interest in the Olympics.

Media in a catch-22

The mediatization of Olympic sports has increased the number of events on the program and invited private broadcasters, seeking exclusive rights to particular events, to raise prices. The IOC insists that a certain amount of TV coverage be universally accessible but leaves enough leeway for content to be locked behind paywalls and subscriptions. Since private broadcasters face enormous problems in recouping the rising expenses in advertising revenues, the IOC is willing to adjust timing and scheduling of events to the need of its media customers. The selection of climbing, surfing, and skateboarding as additional sports at Tokyo 2020 aims at younger audiences from the Global North that are disinterested in conventional sports. Placing the Games into Tokyo's midsummer heat is a bow to the global sport event circuit, as America's Big Four sport leagues and European football are not yet in full-swing. Time slot allocations also follow the money. American broadcaster NBC has been paying to the IOC more than four times per event than the Japan Consortium. The coalition of NHK and private broadcasters paid a record $660 million for exclusive rights for the 2016–2020 Olympiad (with NHK covering about 70%).

Japan's private broadcasters are all part of media networks that were founded by the major newspaper houses, and the four largest broadcasters as well as major regional newspapers have come on-board for Olympic sponsorship. Hence when it comes to troubling issues such as athletes' health in Tokyo's summer heat, corruption scandals, and the economic burden of hosting, the media face a conflict of interest. Should they pay more attention to their corporate sponsors or to the politics of the Games?

On a global scale, critical media reporting has contributed to the demise of the "urban growth myth," which promises purely positive results from hosting mega-events. In recent times, politicians are increasingly confronted with the reluctance of their local electorate to support their ambitions. Citizens in Vienna (2013), Munich (2013), and Hamburg (2015) voted against their governments and forced them to give up on the "Olympic dream," and other cities have also backed out in recent years. The failure of the bid for Tokyo 2016 was largely explained by the IOC's concern about the lackluster enthusiasm among residents. One bid later, the IOC opinion poll displayed a significant increase of support from 55.5% in Tokyo and 53.5% in all Japan to 70% and 67% respectively. A close reading of the media reporting on the two bids reveals their crucial role in manufacturing national consent and framing the central narrative of hosting the Games, with critical reporting drastically declining over the consecutive periods.

Manufacturing national consent

The 2016 bid was spearheaded by Tokyo's controversial Governor Ishihara Shintaro, who ultimately seemed to be the single driving force behind the bid as well as responsible for the critical reactions to his power play from those outside Tokyo. Ishihara also initiated the second bid with its motto, "Discover Tomorrow," but pulled out of local politics before the IOC's decision in 2013. For how the Japanese newspapers reported on winning the bid on September 13, see Figure 2.1. In marked contrast to the earlier bid, the second campaign was re-fashioned as teamwork involving a wide variety of collaborators in the service of national interest, led by Prime Minister Abe Shinzo and his strong nationalist agenda. "All Japan" is a key term that emerged during the second bid campaign. All Japan became a metaphor for the whole nation plus a nickname for the cross-sectional, nation-wide alliance of key persons. Most notable was the successful incorporation of governors from prefectures in Tokyo's neighborhood and the disaster-struck region, as well as the alliance between competing companies as joint sponsors. As a member of the wide-ranging and bipartisan Advisory Board to the Organising Committee, Abe demonstrated his strong involvement at the all-important IOC session with the infamous statement that Tokyo is safe from radiation and his

Figure 2.1 Winning the bid: newspaper headlines September 8, 2013.
Source: © Antje Bieberstein.

flashy appearance at the Rio 2016 Games closing ceremony dressed up as Super Mario.

The shocking experience of the Great East Japan Earthquake and the nuclear disaster was of particular significance in forging a national alliance and streamlining public opinion in the bidding phase. The 2020 bidding campaign built on the emotional appeal of showcasing to the world Japan's recovery after the devastating disasters and cast Tokyo 2020 as the "Recovery Olympics" (*fukkō gorin*). The bid cemented public awareness of the "power of the dream" (of hosting) as being what Japan most needed right now. This promotional slogan effectively minimized the discursive space for public critique or opposition. It maximized support and camouflaged the disproportionally high significance that hosting the Games has for the Greater Tokyo Area, as opposed to the country as a whole. The "power of the dream" resonates with the "power of sports," and was music to the ears of the IOC.

Freedom of speech concerns

Even in the liberal newspaper *Asahi Shimbun*, not known as a supporter of either Ishihara or Abe, critical reporting has been scaled down. The invisibility of opponents, the silencing of critical issues, the paucity of self-reflection are characteristic of media narratives serving the needs of political elites. That we are now in the midst of an "Asian Age," in which Korea, Russia, China, and Middle Eastern nations are in the course of hosting sports mega-events is indicative of a shift away from democratic societies where ruling elites need to seek their voters' compliance. While the control of media reporting in Japan is a far cry from the outright censorship of authoritarian regimes in China or North Korea, the grip by the Japanese state on the media has increased in recent years. Wherever the media are willing to sacrifice neutrality and critical reporting for the privilege of staying in contact with political elites, they are likely to contribute to a sanitized display of seemingly common interests pooled behind the unanimous support for hosting the sports mega-event.

3 Skateboarding

"F*** the Olympics"

Wolfram Manzenreiter

For the IOC, granting skateboarding entry to the Tokyo Olympics was a strategic move to sustain interest in its flagship events among younger generations and new media consumers. "We want to take sport to the youth," explained IOC president Bach. "F*** the Olympics," echoed replies through social media channels. Old-school skaters stick to the idea of skateboarding as essentially a do-it-yourself, unruly and daring counterculture and safe haven for nerds, misfits, and the underprivileged who neither comply with the physique nor the mindset of mainstream sportspeople. For them, Olympic skateboarding is sort of a mixed blessing, at best.

"Street" and "park" competitions at Tokyo 2020 are a joint product by the Fédération Internationale de Roller Sports and the International Skateboarding Federation. Street courses resemble Street League events, featuring rails, hubbas, ledges, stairs, etc. Park competitions take place along steep walls and tricky curves. Judges will rate runs according to difficulty and variety of flips, spins, and height of jumps. Forty male and forty female skateboarders will qualify themselves at major tournaments prior to the Games. Japan is guaranteed four slots. Thirteen-year old world champion Okamoto Misugu or 2017 world champion Nishimura Aori are very likely to enter the competition, assuming they don't get injured. Injuries are part of any skater's biography, no matter what level.

Skateboarding reached Japan in the 1970s. After years of ups and downs, Japan's skateboarding scene now numbers 400,000 skaters. Only a handful can make a living through the sport. About 1,000 pros and amateurs appear annually at the contests sponsored by the three associations governing the sport. The associations also license pro-skaters and judges, train new blood, and link up with the TOCOG. The greatest challenges are the never-ending conflicts between skaters taking over the city as their playground and municipal governments banishing skateboarding from residential and business areas.

Although the Olympic skatepark at the Ariake Urban Sports Venue can't compensate for overall shortage of facilities, it might help mitigate the conflict. Already, on the day of the events, the skatepark will be opened to the general public. This is a noble gesture and great publicity move. It will also have the IOC navigate through a legal minefield, as the TOP sponsors of Olympic sports won't be amused to see the skaters flash out their most preferential brands of wear and gear.

4 Political Games

Axel Klein

"The situation is under control!"

"The Games of the 32nd Olympiad in 2020 are awarded to the city of [some fumbling with the big envelope] … Tokyo!" Every member of the Japanese delegation who had travelled to Buenos Aires in 2013 jumped up from their seats. Prime Minister Abe, head of the ruling Liberal Democrats (LDP) and active part of the campaign, smiled, showing a hint of hugging to his neighbor before being enthusiastically hugged by Japan's then NOC president Takeda Tsunekazu. After its failed bid for 2016, when Tokyo governor Ishihara Shintaro led the endeavor, the Japanese capital had now secured the rights to hold the billion-dollar event.

For Abe this victory also meant that he had convinced a sufficient number of IOC members that, as he put it, "the situation is under control." This referred to Fukushima's nuclear power plant, which had been a major part of the 2011 triple disaster of earthquake, tsunami, and nuclear meltdown, the latter of which contaminated many rural communities with radioactivity and forced about 160,000 Japanese to leave their homes. It had been one of Abe's major talking points in front of the IOC assembly that both the destroyed nuclear power plant and earthquakes would pose no threat to the 2020 Olympic Games in Tokyo.

By far not everyone in Japan shared that sentiment but what else could Abe say? He clearly did not waver: His party had never given up on nuclear energy even though the very close ties of Liberal Democrats to the operators of nuclear power plants had contributed to a momentous lack of oversight and safety measures. Being a country without conventional energy resources to speak of, the LDP argued that in order to maintain a necessary minimum of self-reliance and to keep energy costs low, nuclear energy could not be abandoned. It just needed tighter control. The situation was under control.

Japanese energy companies, which have been enjoying regional monopolies for decades, were by far not the only close business allies of the LDP. Over its many decades of single-party dominance starting in 1955, the Liberal Democrats had fostered close ties to almost all industries, with the deal being industry-friendly policies in exchange for financial support for the ruling party. The basic philosophy of "convoy capitalism" had assigned the role of guardian and supporter of Japanese business interests to the government while the companies would take care of employees and indirectly their families. Women would not be gainfully employed full time but become homemakers, child and senior care included. Employers on the other side would keep jobs secure even during economic downturns. Like a convoy, society as a whole would benefit from this arrangement and move ahead while companies donated generously to the LDP to keep the system going.

The political situation out of control

From 1955 to 1993, no opposition party was able to seriously challenge the LDP. It took a number of unique factors to end the Liberal Democratic dominance: the end of the Cold War, a number of corruption cases involving leading LDP politicians, second and third generation "dynastic" politicians who wanted change, and the consequential bursting of Japan's bubble economy. Also relevant was the fact that convoy capitalism did not allow for globalization, equal opportunity and the advancement of women, free market competition, or a government that gives priority to its citizens and not its companies. The impact of these factors, however, grew stronger in Japan and eventually damaged convoy capitalism considerably.

The resulting pessimism among Japanese overshadowed the 1993 general elections. Many reform-oriented Liberal Democrats had left their party to form new ones and campaigned almost exclusively on reform. And they won. As a result, a seven-party coalition took over government including every party except for the LDP and the Communists. The only common mission that united them, next to the chance of experiencing power, was to reform the rules of the political system, an endeavor usually referred to as "political reform." Then Prime Minister Hosokawa Morihiro stayed in office for less than a year but during that time managed to have a new electoral system, party financing rules and other new laws passed, all of which were supposed to clean up and renew Japanese politics.

Being out of power paralyzed the LDP for a while because the party only knew how to function with access to state resources. Deprived of the state budgets and the ability to make policy decisions, Liberal Democrats were scared to also lose company donations and even more elections. The party therefore worked frantically to regain power. Its leadership shrewdly convinced its former arch enemy, the Socialist Party, to form a coalition and in 1994 re-took control of government. Then it did not take much longer to get rid of the Socialists and in 1995 the LDP was back where it had been for so many decades before: ruling alone. A realistic look at voter behavior, however, made it clear to party leadership that there were more challenges to come in the near future and it negotiated another alliance with a former arch enemy. This time it was Komeito, the "Clean Government Party," established in 1964 by the religious lay organization Soka Gakkai, which for decades had been running on a clear anti-LDP platform. In 1999, both parties formed a coalition, with the declared aim of mutually improving electoral chances.

Only a month before Tokyo's bid for the 2016 Olympics failed in 2009, however, a general election had again drastically changed Japan's political world. The LDP had lost its majority to the Democratic Party of Japan (DPJ), a force that many Japanese apparently voted for to try something different. And that it was. The DPJ ran on the slogan "from concrete to people," meaning that the government should use its resources not for an endless string of infrastructure projects all over the country but direct it to the country's families, employees, and consumers.

Fortunately for the LDP, the DPJ did not govern very well. Three different DPJ politicians tried themselves as Prime Ministers until finally, in 2012, the party suffered a crushing defeat and the LDP, again with its junior coalition partner Komeito, won back power. Never mind that the LDP did not win more votes than in 2009 when it lost. The party simply profited from the apparent frustration of many voters who decided to abstain from voting. The 2012 defeat not only made the DPJ implode but also deflated the hopes in opposition parties for many voters. Even in the year of the Olympics the opposition camp has not recovered, leaving Japanese voters hardly any promising alternative to the LDP. Since 2012, almost half of all eligible voters responded to this choice set with absenteeism. Low voter turnout coupled with a particular mechanism of the electoral system have allowed the LDP to command a comfortable majority of more than 60% of the seats, with only about 16% of all eligible voters actually voting for the party.

Olympics and the constitution

For a national government, Olympic Games offer a lot of opportunities to raise its popularity both at home and abroad. In addition, economic resources can be mobilized and secured to create the infrastructure needed for the big event. Quite a few LDP politicians lined up to somehow profit from the new treasure trove, trying to direct some of that money towards their own constituency. But Abe looked beyond the usual pork barrel dealings, he had a bigger plan. His intention was to make 2020 truly significant for Japan by announcing his intention to reform the country's constitution. Japan's basic law had never been changed since it was written by the US occupational forces after World War II and enacted in 1947. Especially conservatives in Japan repeatedly insist on the need to create a "Japanese" constitution including the traditional values they deem essential for their country. Abe's grandfather, Kishi Nobusuke, had also been Prime Minister (1957–1960) but was unsuccessful in his attempt to reform the constitution. In 2012, Abe started his own campaign. With his ruling coalition commanding a two thirds majority, one important precondition for constitutional reform was secured. The other existed as Abe managed to have a bill passed that set the rules for how to conduct the necessary popular vote on the issue. But then his own camp caused trouble.

Opinions on what and how to change were so diverse within the LDP itself and its support organizations that Abe found himself quickly between a rock and many hard places. Any concrete suggestions would be rejected by at least one influential group of conservative forces, making it virtually impossible after 2012 to come up with an LDP draft. In addition, Komeito proved reluctant to push the issue. Having been established as a pacifist force, Komeito was especially wary of any change that could lead to a more active role of the Japanese military. Pacifism had been at the core of Komeito's self-conception and its voters would not have it any other way.

Not surprisingly, the most contentious reform issue has been Article 9 of the Japanese constitution which declares that "land, sea, and air forces, as well as other war potential, will never be maintained." The same Article, however, has been interpreted in such a way that self-defense is exempted from this restriction, allowing the Japanese government, with support of the US, to establish the Self-Defense Forces (SDF) in 1955, comprising 250,000 "members" and commanding a sophisticated military arsenal. Since the late 1980s, international pressure, especially from the US, has kept Japan on the defensive because of the country's rejection to send troops abroad and participate in military missions. Only slowly did the SDF join UN peacekeeping operations starting in the 1990s – as long as they included no combat.

There is a very vocal pacifist resistance among Japanese who reject any change to – what they call – the "peace constitution," but especially to Article 9. This resistance comprises, among others, political parties on the left, religious organizations, and parts of the liberal political camp. They all share the belief that Abe and his LDP cannot be trusted and that any change of the constitution will be a step on the path to active participation in military aggression. Remember the past, beware the beginnings. Abe, however, leads those who at least want to put the SDF on a constitutionally sound footing. Even Komeito agreed to add to Article 9 in a way that would do away with any legal doubt regarding the constitutionality of the SDF, but then had second thoughts and readjusted its position to "constitutional reform should be discussed carefully from now on."

Abe's term in office ends in 2021. Constitutional reform would by far be the most significant achievement of his long time in power. With the opposition in disarray and a stable parliamentary majority, the year 2020 seems to offer a unique opportunity for the Prime Minister to do something no other Prime Minister has ever achieved before him. In the world of Japanese politics, it may be just this issue that will compete with the Olympics for attention. Let the Games begin.

5   Number Games

The economic impact of Tokyo 2020

Franz Waldenberger

It all depends

Olympic Games are mega-events. They are known to afford "mega" budgets. Still, organizers expect the overall benefits to surmount the costs. However, neither costs nor benefits can be unambiguously measured. It is not just a forecasting problem. Even after the Games, the numbers will be disputed. There is a simple reason for this. In order to correctly assess the costs and benefits, a fundamental question needs to be answered: How would the economy of the host city and country have performed, if they had not hosted the Olympic and Paralympic Games? The economic impact of the Games is then given by comparing the development with and without the Games. The problem is that the all-decisive reference point is purely hypothetical. It cannot be observed. We can only assume what the development without the Games might have been. The numbers change as we vary our assumptions about the "what if." This can also be seen in the case of the Tokyo 2020 Games (see Figure 5.1). Cost estimates vary from $5.2 to $28.1 billion and benefit estimates from $64 to $155 billion. Assessments of the overall economic impact range from $36 to $220 billion.

Costs – allocating public infrastructure investments and budgets

Tokyo's application files submitted to the IOC in January 2013 distinguish three cost categories. (1) The budget of the Tokyo Organising Committee of the Olympic and Paralympic Games (TOCOG), (2) Non-TOCOG capital investments for sports venues, the Olympic Village, and other infrastructure built for the Games, (3) Non-TOCOG operational costs related to services and activities in such areas as security, transportation, medical support or cultural and educational events. The TOCOG budget estimate amounts to $3.4 billion, which is equivalent to 41% of the total

a) Cost estimates in billion US dollar

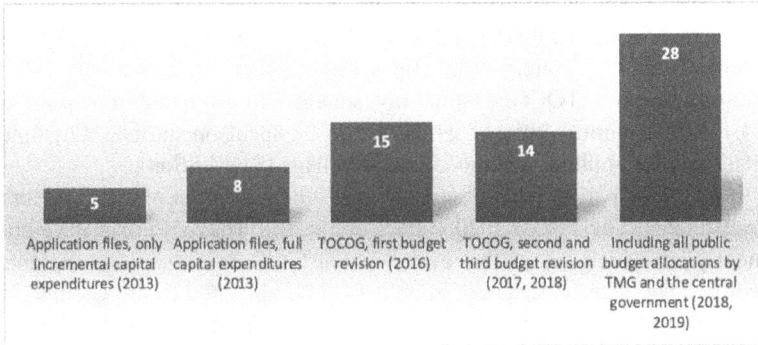

b) Benefit estimates in billion US dollar

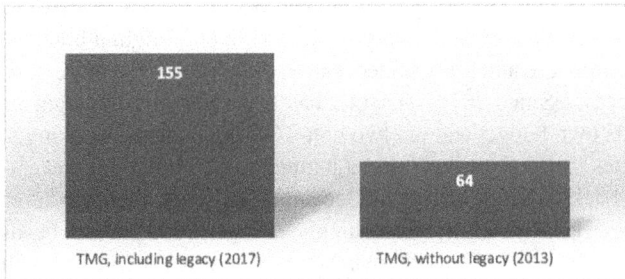

c) Estimates of overall economic impact in billion US dollar

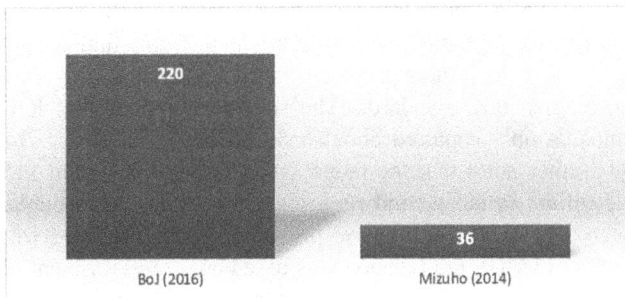

Illustration by the author. Refer to main text for more information and sources.

Figure 5.1 Estimates of costs, benefits, and overall economic impact of the 2020 Games.

budget. Expenditures relate to the promotion, preparation, and operation of the sports events and include rent, wages, and other running costs as well as expenses for all kinds of services like telecommunication or transportation. They are balanced by contributions from the IOC ($0.8 billion), sponsors and official suppliers ($1.3 billion) and by income generated by the Games including mainly ticket sales ($0.8 billion) and licensing ($0.1 billion). The non-TOCOG capital investments are estimated to amount to $4.4 billion, almost 60% of which are to be spent on the new Olympic Stadium ($1.5 billion) and the Olympic Village ($1.1 billion).

One tricky part in the cost assessment is the allocation of infrastructure investments. The Tokyo 2020 Games are part of Tokyo's urban development plan, which means that even without the Games many investments would have been undertaken. Should they be allocated to the Games? If one only includes investments exclusively tied to the hosting of the Games, the related non-TOCOG capital investment estimates come down to $1.8 billion. The total budget would correspondingly be reduced to $5.2 billion, and the share of the TOCOG budget would then be roughly two-thirds.

Olympic Games are known for notoriously exceeding original budgets. Half of the Summer Games organized since 1976 cost 80% more than originally forecast.[1] Since 2016, TOCOG has been annually updating its estimates for its own budget and the two non-TOCOG budgets. Looking at the three updates the total budget figures jumped to $15 billion in December 2016, fell back to $13.5 billion in December 2017 and then remained unchanged in December 2018. Accordingly, Tokyo 2020 would be as expensive as London 2012. The cost overrun of 52% would be in line with Rio 2016 (51%), but still lower than London 2012 (76%).

How can the dramatic revisions in the official Tokyo 2020 budgets be explained? The Board of Audit of Japan, which in October 2018 evaluated the preparations for the Olympics, attributes the jump in the first budget revision to the fact that the figures presented in the application files were calculated according to IOC standards. The statement implies that IOC accounting standards only captured about 55% of the actual costs. The Board of Audit further notes that the reduction of the estimate from $15 billion to $13.5 billion in the second revision is not explained in public documents. According to the information provided by the Tokyo Metropolitan Government (TMG), the revision was based on a re-assessment of public expenditures that had incorrectly been attributed to the Games, although they would have been incurred irrespective of the hosting of the Games. Again, this reveals the uncertainties and in a way the arbitrariness of how public expenditures are allocated. Such revisions, while reducing the estimated public burden, also reduce the credibility of the numbers presented.

To add to the confusion, in January 2018 Koike Yuriko, Governor of Tokyo, announced that the city would put an additional $8.1 billion aside for the Games. Adding this to the $6 billion stated in the TOCOG report, one arrives at costs of $14.1 billion to be borne by the TMG alone, about 20% of the city's general annual budget. In January 2019, Sakurada Yoshitaka, at the time the minister in charge of the Tokyo Olympics, provided new estimates of the central government's total budget for the Games amounting to $2.9 billion, $1.4 billion higher than the budget figures given by the TOCOG report. Even more frightening however are the numbers presented by the Board of Audit of Japan's October 2018 report. The report revealed that various ministries and agencies of the central government had over the four years from April 2013 to March 2018 budgeted expenditures of $8 billion under 286 projects declared to be related to the Games. Updating the cost estimates on the basis of these numbers one arrives at a total amount of $28.1 billion, 3.4 times the original estimate of $8.3 billion.

The extreme range in the numbers related to the public financial burden can be seen to be the outcome of two opposing interests. The IOC and TOCOG want the public budget to appear as small as possible not only to guard against public criticism, but also to not discourage future candidate cities. On the other hand, for the TMG and the ministries of the central government the Games are a window of opportunity to obtain additional budgets. The argument "necessary expenses for the smooth operation of the Games" is likely to sell well in budget negotiations. Also, as disaster relief policy measures show, it is not uncommon to secure higher budgets than eventually needed, as the "unused money" may later be used for other purposes.

"The Oxford Olympic Study 2016," which assesses the costs and cost overruns of Summer and Winter Games from 1960 to 2016 based on official IOC data, finds that Olympic Games have the highest cost overruns compared to any other mega-projects. In their 2014 paper on mega-projects they list many reasons why cost overruns occur: (a) the inherent riskiness and complexity of such projects; (b) the lack of experience of local planners as mega-projects tend to travel across locations; (c) conflicting interests among stakeholders; (d) too high ambitions by organizers; and (e) incentive and misrepresentation problems.[2] The various Tokyo 2020 cost estimates suggest that conflicts of interest between the IOC and the local organizing committee on the one hand and government officials on the other hand regarding how to account for Games-related expenditures represent the most important source for apparent increases in and divergences among estimates.

Benefits – possibly huge, but hard to measure and not evenly spread

Cities apply for the Games because of the benefits they expect from being a host. There are first the infrastructure investments in the run up to the Games. They go beyond the capital expenditures for venues, as they also include construction in anticipation of a rising number of tourists. The Bank of Japan estimates construction investments related to the Games to amount to $100 billion, boosting annual GDP by $220 billion between 2014 and 2020.[3] But to what extent do these investments actually generate additional demand and not just crowd out otherwise undertaken investment? The stimulus can be expected to be largest in the context of high unemployment and unused production capacities. Given Japan's very low rate of unemployment and the strong demand created by the reconstruction of the disaster-hit areas in the Tohoku region, crowding out effects cannot be neglected. The overall economic impact is likely to be smaller than Bank of Japan calculations suggest and more in line with the estimate of $36 billion given by the Mizuho Research Institute.[4] The additional demand will again be lost once the investments are completed. There is then likely to be a downturn.

Of course, the modernized transportation, communication, and tourist infrastructures including barrier-free access to public buildings and transportation and the greening of the cityscape will contribute to the city's economic performance and well-being of citizens and visitors beyond 2020. These effects are not as easy to measure. In 2017, the TMG estimated these legacy effects to amount to $131 billion, more than five times the estimated direct effects ($24 billion).[5] This sounds rather optimistic. Given the high level of sophistication of Tokyo's existing infrastructure, upgrading effects should be marginal. In the end, these benefits will also depend on whether Tokyo will be able to continue to attract international events and foreign visitors to keep the occupancy rates at a level high enough to generate economic surplus. This is even more pressing because population decline, which already began nationwide since 2010, is predicted to reach Tokyo after 2020.

Tourism is not only a factor feeding into infrastructure investments. It is also an important benefit channel by itself. Visitors bring money. During the Games, 920,000 spectators are expected to stay in Tokyo. Like with investments, the question is to what extent they crowd out tourists who would otherwise have come. Given the additional accommodation capacities newly built or provided through for example Airbnb, crowding out might not be expected. But Japan has over the last seven years experienced an almost fourfold increase in the number of visitors from abroad, from

8.4 million in 2012 to 31.2 million in 2018, mainly from China and other countries in East and Southeast Asia. The main reasons for Japan's tourist boom are rising income levels in the region, a cheap yen, the growth of low-cost carriers, and improved diplomatic relations combined with policies to promote tourism both in Japan and in the countries of origin.

Although the Tokyo 2020 Games have been receiving the full backing from the Japanese government, it would be wrong to equate Tokyo with Japan. The Games are likely to increase the disparities in economic and cultural activities between the capital and Japan's regions and this constitutes probably the largest downside. Official documents avoid mentioning this aspect, but it cannot be neglected in an overall assessment of the economic impact of the Games.

Changing perceptions and mindsets

After all, the most important value of the Games for Tokyo and Japan might not be the new infrastructures or the additional tourists. The overarching theme postulated by the city's application was "Discover Tomorrow." The TOCOG slogan emphasizes the power of sport to promote diversity and positive change. Like in 1964, when Japan proudly presented itself to the world as a rapidly advancing nation, 2020 will be used to showcase new technology and environmental initiatives, to demonstrate Japanese culture and hospitality, and to position Japan's capital as a safe and secure place where people from all over the world can meet and engage in mutually beneficial exchange. The motto reaches out to the world, but it also addresses the Japanese population, especially the younger generation, by creating awareness about not only the necessity, but also the benefits of international exchange and diversity. The Games are seen as a window of opportunity to change perceptions and mindsets both at home and abroad and to rejuvenate an aging society and economy by inviting the world to Tokyo and Japan. If such change can be set in motion, the benefits will indeed be huge, though not easily expressed in numbers.

Notes

1 Flyvbjerg, Bent, Allison Stewart, Alexander Budzier. 2016. "The Oxford Olympics Study 2016: Cost and cost overrun at the Games." *Saïd Business School Research Paper* 2016(20).
2 Flyvbjerg, Bent. 2014. "What you should know about megaprojects and why: An overview." *Project Management Journal* 45(2): 6–19.
3 Osada, Mitsuhiro, et al. 2016. "Economic impact of the Tokyo 2020 Olympic Games." *BoJ Reports & Research Papers*, January. www.boj.or.jp/en/research/brp/ron_2016/ron160121b.htm/.

4 Mizuho Research Institute. 2014. "The economic impact of the 2020 Tokyo Olympic Games." *Mizuho Economic Outlook & Analysis*, October 17.
5 Bureau of Olympic and Paralympic Games Tokyo 2020 Preparation. 2017. "Tōkyō 2020 taikai kaizai ni tomonau keizai hakyū kōka" [Economic impact of the Tokyo 2020 Games] www.2020games.metro.tokyo.lg.jp/9e1525ac4c454d17 1c82338c5a9b4c8a_1.pdf.

6   Climbing

New sport on the block

Wolfram Manzenreiter

Climbing has come a long way since its inception by Victorian mountaineers and local guides in the European Alps. For most of its history, the sheer idea of competitions and indoor climbing was a sacrilege to many that celebrated mountain climbing as a "brotherhood of the rope" and life-transcending quest in the wilderness. Risk-reducing devices, grading standards, and artificial climbing walls in urban gyms facilitated the transformation into a sport of its own and the emergence of a colorful subculture with its own media, brands, and celebrities.

The Japan Mountaineering and Sport Climbing Association (JMSCA, until 2017 just JMA) is in charge of sport climbing, including the execution of rules, judging, licensing, and contests. About 550 climbing gyms are in operation in Japan, about 100 in Tokyo alone. User fees are moderate, and the sport is easy to learn and fascinating to watch. Climbing requires physical strength and agility, as well as mental strength and imagination in how to solve a problem on the climbing wall. Top athletes can challenge problems side-by-side with children or seniors.

International tournaments have been a vital part of sport climbing since the 1990s. The International Federation of Sport Climbing (IFSC) oversees championships and cup tournaments in three distinctive categories for men and women. In lead climbing, athletes climb up a vertical route as high as possible. Speed climbing is basically a head-to-head race along a fixed route on a ten or 15-meter wall; in bouldering, climbers tackle as many technically challenging routes as possible on a four-meter wall. At Tokyo 2020, 20 men and women compete in all disciplines. Aggregated results determine the ultimate ranks. Qualifiers are taking place at three tournaments in the lead-up to the Games; two slots are guaranteed to Japan, and two are bestowed on invitees.

Climbing's Olympic debut in 2020 is no surprise when the host's ambitions for gold are taken into consideration. In the past four World Cup seasons, Japan won the team competition. As of June 2019, 15 of the world's top 50 male lead climbers are Japanese (and nine among women); in bouldering, five of the top ten male climbers are Japanese (women: three). Veteran world champions are Narasaki Tomoa and Noguchi Akiyo, and at the 2018 Youth Olympics in Buenos Aires that introduced the combined event, gold and silver went to Japan's Dohi Keita and Tanaka Shuta.

7 Advertising the Games

Sponsoring a new era

Isaac Gagné

In the 21st century, the Olympic Games showcase not just the athletic prowess of athletes from around the world, but also corporate marketing savviness. With the highest sponsorship revenue in the history of the Games, estimated at nearly the entire sponsorship revenue of the previous three Summer Games combined,[1] Tokyo 2020 is shaping up to be a record-breaking showcase of corporate sponsorship and global sports marketing. At the center of this multi-billion-dollar marketing machine is the global advertising powerhouse Dentsu Corporation, which is behind Olympic marketing for both individual corporations and the Tokyo Olympics itself.

However, the lucrative world of Olympic sponsorship and sports marketing, and Dentsu's central role in this multi-billion-dollar industry, is a relatively recent development. This chapter draws from first-hand insights from Ebizuka Osamu, a sports marketing expert who joined Dentsu in 1974 and was on the front lines of Olympic marketing from the 1980s into the 2000s.[2] Ebizuka's insights reveal that until the 1980s the Olympics and Paralympics were mostly viewed as little more than an expensive PR opportunity for host cities and a risky investment for companies. However, a culmination of innovative Olympic developments and bold risk-taking by companies transformed the Olympic Games into a sports marketing extravaganza of unrivaled proportions.

Dentsu and the Olympics: Tokyo 1964 to LA 1984

In the lead-up to Japan's first Olympics in 1964, there was no Olympics division at Dentsu. Instead, they dispatched 15 people to Tokyo's Olympic Organizing Committee (OOC, the equivalent to today's Organising Committee of the Olympic and Paralympic Games). According to Ebizuka, the Olympic Games were not considered a particularly valuable opportunity from the perspective of Japanese companies. Broadcasting rights for Tokyo 1964 were the sole property of the national broadcaster NHK, although private commercial broadcaster Nippon Television also joined in the Olympics coverage. Dentsu was in charge of public relations for the Games, but it did not go much beyond posters and limited radio and television ads, and a souvenir book funded by ads from 100 or so local companies. In other words, the 1964 Tokyo Olympic Games were barely on the radar of the corporate world.

Up until the 1980s, the Olympics and Paralympics were gatherings of amateur athletes shouldered almost entirely by public money from the respective host cities, and sponsorships were not a major revenue stream. Yet as the Games expanded in scope throughout the 1950s, 1960s, and 1970s, hosting the mega-event became increasingly costly, culminating in massive debt for the 1976 Montreal Olympics. In the lead-up to the 1984 Summer Games in Los Angeles, over 80% of LA residents opposed the Games. However, city officials promised not to use any public funds. In addition to selling exclusive broadcasting rights based on competitive bidding (previously rights had been sold directly to broadcasters), the previous ban on the participation of professional athletes was lifted to generate revenue and public interest. The result was that the 1984 Los Angeles Olympics and Paralympics were the first completely privatized Summer Games. Although corporate sponsorship had been used in the past, the emphasis on competitive bidding for licensing and sponsorship helped make the Los Angeles Olympics and Paralympics the first in history to come out in the black, and 55% of the revenue came from broadcasting rights and sponsorship fees. Thus, a new era of monetized Olympic Games marketing began.

With the privatization and monetization of the Olympic Games, Dentsu's role in global sports marketing took shape. In fact, Dentsu was one of the early companies to identify the possibilities of corporate sponsorship for sports marketing, and in 1982 Dentsu teamed up with Adidas' Horst Dassler to create the joint venture sports marketing company International Sports and Leisure (ISL) to develop marketing and sponsorship strategies for international sports federations such as the international soccer association FIFA and the international track and field association IAAF.

Dentsu was also active in recruiting corporate sponsors for the 1984 Los Angeles Summer Games. At the time, there was no system of National Olympic Committees (NOCs) yet to manage domestic rights during Olympic Games, and there was also no worldwide sponsorship system. Instead, most companies negotiated independently for advertising rights in various domestic markets, such as Mitsubishi Motors and Nikon's sponsorship deals for the 1984 Sarajevo Winter Olympics. However, for the 1984 Los Angeles Summer Games, acting as the sole advertising agent for the majority of Japan's large companies, Dentsu was able to secure marketing rights for Japanese companies such as Mitsubishi, Nikon, Fujifilm,

Brother, and Sanyo among others. 1984 marked a new era of marketing for the Olympic Games, and it also heralded a new era for Dentsu's entry into worldwide sports marketing.

Dentsu and the development of worldwide Olympic sponsorship

The success of the 1984 Summer Olympics signaled what marketing executive and Olympic chronicler Michael Payne called the "Olympic Turnaround" in his eponymous 2005 book. However, it was not enough to convince Japanese companies of the possibilities of global sports marketing. By the mid-1980s Ebizuka was deeply engaged with Dentsu's global sports marketing activities, and he described this period as an extremely difficult time to recruit sponsors for the upcoming 1988 Seoul Olympics. As he explained, in the 1980s Japanese companies still saw the Olympics as a risky investment, and this was doubly so for an Olympics held in Seoul where Japanese products were not even allowed into South Korean markets. Japanese companies felt that there was no merit in attaching their names to the Olympics.

On the other hand, globally the movement toward corporate sponsorship was gaining momentum. By 1985, ISL secured marketing rights from the International Olympic Committee (IOC) and began to recruit companies to become worldwide Olympic partners, a program that became known as TOP – The Olympic Partners. Still, in the 1980s Olympic sponsorship was no guaranteed goldmine. Ebizuka, who worked closely with ISL during this time, recalled how hard Dentsu labored in those early days to recruit Japanese sponsors. In fact, the first Japanese worldwide sponsor Panasonic became involved more or less accidentally. After an aborted attempt to sponsor a football tournament with ISL in Europe, at a business dinner an ISL official suggested that Panasonic try sponsoring the Olympics. As a result, Dentsu negotiated with the IOC to create an audiovisual category to accommodate Panasonic, while ISL negotiated for Philips to join the television category. In the end, these two rival companies shared similar product categories in the first TOP program.

After Panasonic became the first Japanese worldwide Olympic sponsor in 1987 (see Figure 7.1), with the assistance of Dentsu, Japanese companies have become increasingly involved in Olympic sponsorship at global and national levels. In addition, compared with the 15 Dentsu employees involved in Olympics marketing in 1964, in 2019 Dentsu's sports marketing department consisted of three divisions with over 300 people, with 100 employees dispatched to Tokyo's Organising Committee of the Olympic and Paralympic Games (OCOG).

Figure 7.1 Panasonic, Japan's first worldwide Olympic sponsor.
Source: © Wolfram Manzenreiter.

Tokyo 2020: manufacturing the myth of "All Japan"

The development of the sponsorship system continued to expand, and today it is a global marketing phenomenon worth billions of dollars. For TOP companies, industry categories and contract terms are decided by the IOC, and they are limited to one company per industry. However, domestic sponsorship rules are at the discretion of respective NOCs. According to Ebizuka, this means that most Olympics and Paralympics organizing committees use conventional bidding competitions among domestic rivals to secure the highest sponsor revenue.

Tokyo 2020, however, represented a new kind of bidding among sponsors. In contrast to competitive bidding for exclusive industry rights by a single company, the JOC announced to the IOC that it was opening the field for joint sponsorship within the same industry. The JOC also mandated that all corporate sponsors had to sponsor both the Olympics and the Paralympics, which was also a break from previous separate sponsorship contracts.

The result was an unprecedented expansion in sponsors and revenue. In fact, this was partially tied to the March 11, 2011 Great East Japan Earthquake and resulting tsunami and nuclear disaster, which spurred the idea for a new marketing campaign from the JOC to increase public support and corporate sponsorship. Japan made its bid for the 2020 Olympics only months after the 2011 disaster, and the JOC felt the need to build national support for the Olympics. The JOC developed the slogan "All Japan" to meet this goal, and Dentsu was tasked with creating the PR campaign for the public and in courting companies as sponsors.

Despite Dentsu's leading role in recruiting sponsors, Ebizuka described the JOC's "All Japan" strategy as a difficult one to market. First of all, the term itself was problematic. He remarked, "'All Japan' does not exist – there are many regions in Japan, and the 2020 Olympics are in Tokyo, not in Osaka or Tohoku," adding that these other regions had a strong sense of rivalry vis-à-vis Tokyo. Second, "All Japan" was meant to go beyond sports-related companies as sponsors. It was a challenge to recruit such companies to get involved in Olympic sponsorship, as well as to get competing companies to become joint sponsors, such as Japan's two airlines, Japan Airlines and All Nippon Airlines, Japan's two major security companies ALSOK and SECOM, and even banks like Mizuho and Mitsui-Sumitomo. The secret to success, according to Ebizuka, was not creating incentives to join, but to create disincentives *not* to join. "All Japan" was a slogan that implicitly meant that if you were not on board, you were not "for Japan." Moreover, he explained that the slogan played on two distinctive qualities of Japanese companies: (1) a tendency for risk-aversion to avoid being criticized for not joining like other companies, and (2) the capacity for traditional rivals to set aside competition in favor of working towards a larger goal (what Ebizuka called "passive patriotism").

Ebizuka emphasized that this would be unthinkable in the US, where companies would compete for marketing rights. The American model, such as that used in the 1984 Los Angeles Olympics, aimed for high revenue through pushing companies to bid higher for exclusive rights. For Tokyo 2020, Dentsu courted companies by offering to split sponsorship costs among multiple companies within the same industry, thereby securing high revenues while also reducing the investment by individual companies. The result was a win-win of companies gaining access to Olympic marketing rights and the JOC raising unprecedented revenues from across the corporate world. Indeed, this was a strategy only possible thanks to Dentsu's ability to play both sides as both the Olympic marketer for the JOC and the sole marketing agent for the majority of Japan's major corporations.

The contemporary corporate sponsorship structure

Three and a half decades after corporate sponsorship first took root, the contemporary Olympic sponsorship system has developed into a complex marketing machine. Today there are three holders of Olympic marketing rights: the International Olympic Committee (IOC), the Organising Committee for the Olympic Games (OCOG) in charge of each specific Games, and the National Olympic Committees (NOCs). There are also domestic Official Suppliers (aka Official Supporters) who have exclusive contracts with the respective OCOG/NOC. Sponsorship is based on contracts with one of these rights holders, and each rank requires different sponsorship costs for the company and comes with successively restricted marketing rights. The number of sponsoring companies differs each Olympiad, as do the costs for sponsorship at each rank.

At the highest level, companies can become Worldwide Olympic Sponsors through contracts with the IOC, known as The Olympic Partners (TOP). There are currently 13 TOP, including three Japanese companies: Bridgestone, Panasonic, and Toyota. Tokyo 2020 features the highest number of TOP, up from 11 in both London 2012 and Rio 2016. Next, Tier 1 Gold Partners (or Gold Sponsors) sign with the OCOG in product categories that do not compete with TOP companies. There are 15 Japanese Gold Partners, the highest number ever, including Asahi Beer, Fujitsu, and Mizuho Financial Group. Tier 2 Official Partners are companies with more restricted marketing rights compared to Gold Sponsors. Tokyo 2020 Tier 2 sponsors include a record-breaking 32 companies, including both of Japan's largest airlines, Japan Airlines (JAL) and All Nippon Airways (ANA) and four of Japan's largest newspapers. Tier 3 sponsors are companies that provide necessary goods and services for the Games. There are 17 Official Suppliers for Tokyo 2020.

Altogether, the unprecedented scale of sponsorship for Tokyo 2020 is a culmination of decades of Olympic commercialization and the particular competitive yet cooperative corporate culture in Japan. It is also a testament to Dentsu's unrivaled corporate connections and sports marketing expertise which continue to evolve in the lucrative world of global sports marketing.[3]

Notes

1 Fujimoto, Junya. 2019. "Supōtsu māketingu no gainen to Nihon no genjō" [The concept of sports marketing and the current situation in Japan]. *Ad Studies* 67: 36–41.
2 Special thanks to Mr. Ebizuka for his insights.
3 For more on sports marketing, see: Ebizuka, Osamu. 2017. *Sports strategies from a marketing perspective.* Tokyo: Sōbun Kikaku.

8 Karate

Bowing to the Olympics in style

Wolfram Manzenreiter

Karate makes its debut as Olympic sport on home ground – not to the unanimous delight of its global followership. Many regard karate as a martial art of self-defense, not a competitive sport belittling its spiritual depth. Yet the popular identification with Japanese philosophy and etiquette is a "modern invention." Karate originates from Chinese body techniques that reached Okinawa long before Japan annexed the former kingdom in 1879. Only when it was refashioned along the lines of other martial arts, karate gained wider acceptance throughout Japan in the early-20th century. After World War II, Occupation Forces helped spread the art abroad. Hollywood has to take the blame for the creation of karate's distorted Orientalist image.

The World Karate Federation (WKF) has more than 190 national members and boasts over a hundred million karateka around the globe. The Japan Karatedo Federation only acknowledges the schools of Shotokan (about 500,000 members), Wado-ryu, Shito-ryu, and Goju-ryu (100,000 each). Then there is a large pool of traditional and full contact karate styles, sporting their own schools, associations, and worldwide networks. Styles differ largely, and quarrels about legitimate forms, techniques, and rules substantially delayed the acknowledgement as Olympic sport ever since first attempts were made in the 1970s.

Tokyo 2020 features 80 female and male athletes, competing in *kata* (form) and *kumite* (sparring) events. The former is a solo performance of strikes and blocks, chosen from 98 officially recognized forms. For the latter, the WKF conflated its established five weight categories into three. Points depend on power, precision, and quality of form of punches and kicks athletes land on their opponents' body. Results from the most important tournaments ahead of the Games determine entries. Host nation Japan is entitled to a maximum of eight representatives with one in each category. Japan's team was the most successful at the 2018 world championships, and Kiyuna Ryo and Shimizu Kiyo are two of the men's and women's WKF champions.

The competition is run at the Mecca of martial arts, the Nippon Budokan. Originally built for the judo tournament at the 1964 Olympics, the octagonal facility is also known for staging concerts and hosting world acts such as The Beatles, Oasis, or Janet Jackson.

Karate's bow to the Olympics however evoked a snippy nod: In February 2019, the IOC decided to scratch karate from the program of Paris 2024.

9   Herculean efforts

What the construction of the Olympic Stadium reveals about working conditions in Japan[1]

Steffen Heinrich

Newspaper reports draw the picture of a city in the midst of a building frenzy. Construction works are so relentless, one correspondent[2] writes, that repeatedly the small pathway leading to the entrance of his hotel is torn down by mistake. The walls of his hotel room exhibit multiple cracks caused by relentless vibrations from a neighboring building site. Other reports illustrate the human toll of a rushed construction effort: a driver of a government minister dies when passing below a brand-new piece of elevated freeway that suddenly crashes onto the road below. The year is 1964 and Tokyo's first-ever Summer Olympics is just a few months away. Fast forward to the spring of 2019, 55 years later and more than a year ahead of the 2020 Games, and things could hardly look more different. Passing by the construction site of the new stadium one finds work is unfolding in a busy but surprisingly quiet manner. Despite its size and central location, streets around the construction site remain spotlessly clean, with dumper trucks entering and exiting the site guided calmly by a group of neatly dressed and helmeted security personnel. Whenever the need arises, the men and women in uniform step out into the street and politely ask bypassing traffic for patience. On Sundays, construction is on hold and car traffic banned from a large section of the road around the stadium, giving visitors and residents some rare inner-city space for leisurely walks and cycling.

The construction of the new stadium as a symbol of Japanese work-styles

Olympic Games are often seen as an opportunity for a country to showcase its social and economic advancement, and Olympic stadiums are often widely recognized iconic symbols of this effort. Comparing the construction of the first and second Tokyo Games therefore suggests that a lot has been achieved in the past 50 years. Yet the new stadium is also symbolic in other rather less admirable respects,[3] in particular in regards to the working conditions of workers involved in its construction. These received international attention due to the suicide of a construction worker in 2017. Many structural problems of the construction sector are known to contribute to such tragedies, yet often these are mere amplifications of issues that plague work in Japan more generally. This applies, for example, to working hours which still rank among the longest in the industrialized world for full-time employees. Most construction workers barely get a full day off a week, and compared to other industries they are most at risk of falling victim to so-called deaths from overwork (*karōshi*) and suicides related to overwork (*karō jisatsu*).

Like Japan's economy as a whole, construction workers have not seen any significant wage growth since the end of the era of high economic growth in the early 1990s, known as the "bubble economy." Three decades later, public and private investments in buildings are still a third below their peak in 1993. Construction then accounted for 8.2% of GDP and employed over 10% of all workers, but this has since fallen to 5.6% and 7% respectively. In Tokyo, where construction sites seem ubiquitous, it can be difficult to comprehend that the industry is in trouble. Investment related to the Olympics has even led to a small boom in building activities. However, the Olympic boom likely even exacerbated some structural problems such as labor shortages. The workforce in the sector is already 23% smaller than in 2000, while the working age population has shrunk by 12% in the same period.

Excessive working hours

Though it is hardly surprising that work in construction can be hard and hazardous, established work-styles clearly constitute additional risks for workers' well-being. The aforementioned suicide of the 26-year-old foreman at the new Olympic Stadium site in 2017 is a case in point (see Figure 9.1 for an aerial view of the construction site of the stadium). Tasked with overseeing the work of ground reinforcement at the new stadium, the worker faced pressure from the overtime-prone work organization and planning delays resulting from the decision to replace the original design for the stadium a year after Tokyo was awarded the Games. Until his death he worked over 200 hours of overtime in a month, well above the 80 hours a month limit that had been set by the government as the "*karōshi* threshold," above which deaths and suicides are treated as potentially caused by overwork.

Although the man's employer claimed to have been unaware of the situation, surveys suggest that this worker's experience is anything but exceptional. The average monthly overtime for workers at building sites has

Figure 9.1 Construction site of the Olympic Stadium, 2015.
Source: © k.2288r102hn8r, Flickr.

been steady above the 80-hours mark for years. After 2017 it fell to 64 hours, potentially a reaction to the massive public interest the case had generated. However, a 2019 report by the international trade union association of construction workers (BWI) suggests that little has changed.[4]

Dual labor market structure

This begs the question why firms are still able to put workers under such pressure given that labor shortages should make it easier for workers to leave high-pressure assignments for jobs with better working conditions. One factor to consider here is the dualistic nature of Japanese employment practices. This concerns, first of all, the relationship between large contractors and subcontractors. A handful of contractors dominate the Japanese construction market, but they employ only few people directly. Much of the work is contracted out to small subcontractors with whom the large contractors negotiate fixed price structures. This makes it difficult for the subcontractors to pay higher wages. Similar patterns are found in other industries with many small and medium-sized suppliers being dependent on a small number of key clients. As a result, small- and medium-sized suppliers tend to have much less room for improving working conditions. This explains some of the substantial differences in the working conditions between large and small firms in Japan.

Another feature of dualistic employment practices concerns the use of so-called non-regular workers. Today 38% of all employees in Japan are non-regularly employed. Most of these jobs come with low pay, limited prospects for career advancement and below-average social security coverage. In construction, many workers are self-employed or temp agency workers. For both, prospects of ever switching to permanent employment are slim. They also have almost no trade union representation as most unions do not cater to non-regular or self-employed workers. Even for standard employees, unionization rates are low in international comparison. This glaring lack of bargaining power in combination with the high share of non-regular workers has prompted the former Tokyo bureau chief of the International Monetary Fund (IMF) to conclude that in Japan employers have "too much power." For him this is the main reason why real wage growth has been flat for almost 30 years[5] – unlike in almost all other OECD member states.

Labor shortages, migrant labor, and informal work

In theory, labor shortages, which have been felt by employers in construction much earlier than in other sectors, could be a factor that improves the bargaining power of workers and thus working conditions. Yet employers have countered such pressures by, among other strategies, recruiting cheap labor from abroad. Until the 1990s this often involved informal and illegal forms of employment, but today several legal options exist. For example, temporary migrant workers from developing countries can enter Japan under the Technical Intern Training Program (TITP) – officially to acquire skills and knowledge while in Japan. Allowing for a maximum of five years of employment in Japan, the TITP functions mostly as a guest worker scheme. Though legally employed and formally covered by the provisions of Japanese labor law, technical trainees do not have the right to bargain and cannot easily switch to another employer. Hence, they have few means to exert influence on their working conditions. The high number of violations against the labor code that authorities unearth every year further illustrates the precarious situation of these workers.

Demand for them, however, is growing inexorably. In official statistics, the number of foreign construction workers has tripled between 2014 and 2019 alone. In part, they replace the dwindling number of Japanese day laborers (*hiyatoi rōdōsha*) who were hugely important in the postwar construction boom and who form a hyper-flexible but often precarious workforce with little social security and employment stability. Although Japanese day laborer traditionally live in specific areas called *yoseba* such as San'ya in Tokyo, whereas the foreign workforce is much more physically dispersed, their economic roles and casual modes of employment with low social security are similar.

Why labor shortages do not always lead to higher wages

Though standard labor economics suggests otherwise, the Olympic-related labor shortages do not necessarily improve the bargaining position of workers. On the contrary, indications are that instead pressure on workers has increased. For example, the bulk of applications for the recognition of *karōshi* stem from sectors that have been hit particularly hard by the shrinking workforce: care work, social services, shipping, and construction.[6]

It would be wrong, however, to assume that the problems described here are not well known or are being ignored by the government. It is with regard to implementation that policymakers appear conspicuously inconsequential. Many recent reforms seem highly sympathetic to workers yet are ambiguous at best in their implications. One example is a scheme for migrant workers (*tokutei ginō no zairyū shikaku*). In force since April 2019, this scheme guarantees migrant workers the same working conditions to comparable Japanese workers. It also offers, for the first time, the prospect of permanent residence. Yet analysts are skeptical that the law is strong enough to enable migrant workers to achieve equal pay for equal work. Another example is a 2018 law designed to cut excessive overtime; even under the new rules, overtime can – under certain conditions – exceed the *karōshi* threshold. Moreover, construction and other sectors where overtime is particularly problematic are exempted from even this reform for five years. Despite strong rhetoric to the contrary, government policy does little to bolster the bargaining position of workers.

In a similar vein, the construction industry readily acknowledges that working conditions need to improve drastically, not least to overcome labor shortages. Yet at present, the industry claims the Olympics are so exceptional that any attempt at change has to wait until after 2020. Given the long history of labor shortages and problematic employment practices in the sector, it seems improbable, however, that the industry will ever feel ready to improve working conditions on its own. In this regard, the construction of the new stadium offers a sobering tale for anyone hoping that demographic aging will quasi-automatically strengthen the market power of workers.

Notes

1 The author thanks Annika Clasen and René Muschter for their assistance.
2 Stadlmann, Heinz. 1964. "Tokio. Das Schlagwort heißt: Rechtzeitig bis zur Olympiade." [Tokyo. Motto is to be punctual for the Olympics]. *Frankfurter Allgemeine Zeitung*, May 2.
3 On the site's symbolism see also Tsutomu, Tomotsune. 2019. "Making heterogeneous space: Land development and the proletarianization of urban underclass in post war Japan." *International Journal of Japanese Sociology* 28(1): 67.
4 Available at www.bwint.org/web/content/cms.media/1542/datas/dark%20side %20report%20lo-res.pdf.
5 Cited in Nohara, Yoshiaki, Brett Miller. 2016. "IMF sees Japanese talent locked in low-paying jobs." *Japan Times*. September 29.
6 Tsuchitani-Watson, Jeremy. 2018. "Karōshi, karō jisatsu, and gender discrimination: Japan's human rights violations." *Asian-Pacific Law & Policy Journal* 19(2): 142–193.

10 Tokyo 2020 and neighborhood transformation

Reworking the entrepreneurial city

Ralph Lützeler

Shortly after Tokyo had been selected as host city of the 2020 Summer Olympics and Paralympics, newspapers all over the world covered the sad story of an elderly citizen named Jinno Kohei. While already being relocated once due to construction activities related to the 1964 Olympics, he – together with another 200 households living in the Kasumigaoka public apartment complex – was asked to move again, this time to make way for the expanded site of the rebuilt Olympic Stadium.

Evictions or displacements of residents are among the usual concomitants of redevelopment projects related to mega-events. It is said that 720,000 people had to move in preparation for the 1988 Seoul Olympics, while the 1996 Atlanta Olympics caused 30,000 residents to leave their homes.[1] To oppose such forced relocations is often like fighting against windmills. Not only huge financial interests are involved but mega-events are also usually part of a top-priority regional or even national strategy to strengthen the economic base of urban regions, known as "entrepreneurial city politics."

This chapter provides a rough estimate on the extent of residential displacement related to the 2020 Olympics. I show that neighborhood transformation in Tokyo is characterized less by direct and conflict-ridden evictions than by indirect, gradual, and spatially isolated forms of residential displacement. The decision to host the 2020 Olympics in Tokyo has accelerated the pace of ongoing urban transformation but has not changed its basic character, nor has it initiated any major residential redevelopment project apart from the Olympic Village complex. Tokyo is a far cry from being a socially just city, but the peculiar features of the real estate market – and not the often-alleged "equality" of Japanese society – mitigate the forces of residential displacement inherent in entrepreneurial city politics even when mega-events such as the Olympic Games are involved.

Tokyo: a dynamic entrepreneurial city surrounded by decline

Entrepreneurial city politics is a technical term for a shift away from the long-standing managerial role of local governments to provide services, facilities, and benefits to urban citizens. Instead, cities opt for economic growth strategies focusing on the attraction of "external sources of funding, new direct investment, or new employment sources." This policy shift started in the United States in the 1970s, when cities faced the threats of deindustrialization, fiscal constraints, and being surpassed by competing municipalities or regions. The lack of resources to realize economic restructuring on their own account induces city administrations to form public-private partnerships with investors that were granted incentives such as the abolition or weakening of city planning standards, tax exemptions, or the bargain sale of public space – including public housing. To improve the competitive edge of urban areas, "consumer attractions (sports stadia, convention and shopping centers, marinas, exotic eating places) and entertainment (the organization of urban spectacles on a temporary or permanent basis)," have become important elements of urban development strategies.[2]

In Japan, entrepreneurial city politics became finally established when Prime Minister Koizumi (2001–2006) started running the government. In direct response to the increasing international competition among metropolises to attract global finance and business functions, and inspired by the British urban renaissance strategy, the Japanese National Diet passed a Law on Special Measures for Urban Renaissance that became effective in April 2002. This law enabled exemptions from building regulations, abridged permit procedures as well as state-secured interest-free loans and guarantees to be implemented in designated special urban redevelopment districts. In the case of Tokyo, it is intended to both support the repopulation of the city center (by upper-middle class citizens) and attract foreign investors and expatriates to successfully compete with other global cities.

This strong focus on the regeneration of Tokyo has without doubt contributed to the fact that the Japanese capital and its neighboring prefectures are now an island of growth surrounded by a sea of shrinking regions. Since the latter half of the 2000s, population figures for all Japan are on a downward trend due to low birth rates and equally low immigration of foreigners. The commuter belt of Tokyo, i.e. the four prefectures of Saitama, Chiba, Tokyo, and Kanagawa, however, showed an increase from 33.4 million inhabitants in 2000 to 36.6 million in 2019 (an increase of 9.6% in relative terms). The core city (i.e., the 23-special-ward area extending over

just 628 km²) absorbed almost half of this increase by growing from 8.1 to
9.6 million residents (17.6%), and this trend is forecasted to continue at
least for another ten to 15 years. The map of Tokyo wards (see Figure
10.1) further reveals that growth was strongest in the central wards where
most designated redevelopment districts are situated. When Tokyo was
selected in 2013 to host the Olympics, the construction of high-
specification office space and luxury residential towers accelerated and
resulted in further population increase, after having experienced a short
slump due to the world financial crisis in 2008/9 and the immediate aftereffects of Japan's 2011 triple disaster.

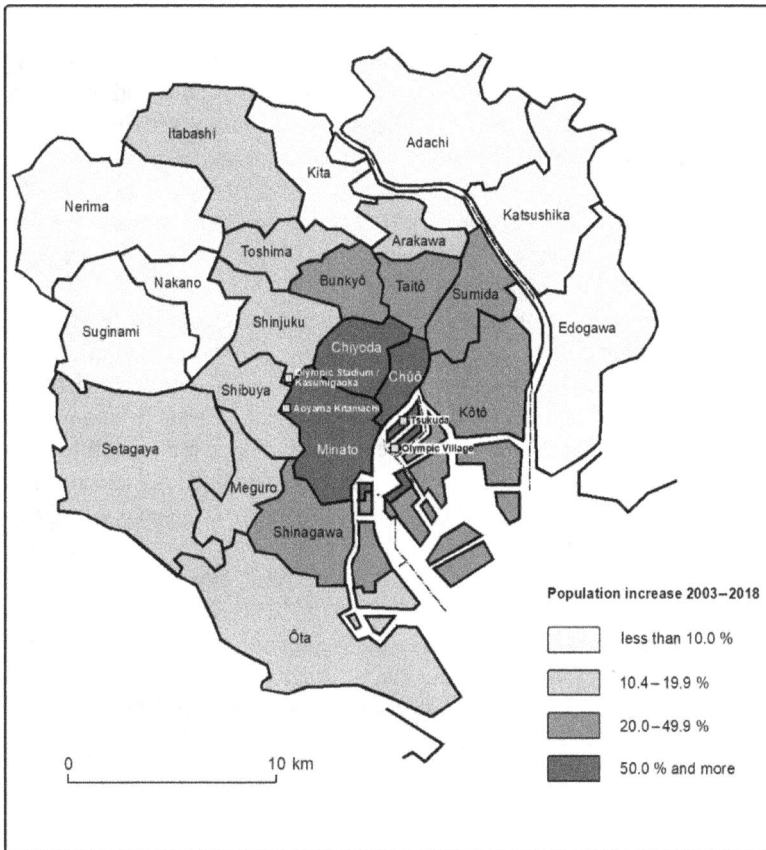

Figure 10.1 Tokyo's population increase 2003–2018 by wards.
Source: Map designed by author.

Evicted in rare cases, but not abandoned: tenants in public housing complexes

Dynamic urban redevelopment of this scale might lead to the assumption that residential displacement is widespread in Tokyo. However, this is not the case. First of all, public housing complexes like the Kasumigaoka estate are an exceptional case. Only here Japanese public authorities, in this case the Tokyo Metropolitan Government (TMG), have the power to evict residents. This power is, however, only rarely used against poor households.

Actually, many public housing complexes, which were built during the heyday of the postwar economic miracle, are now in a dilapidated state and beyond repair. In the case of rebuilding, all former tenants still eligible for public housing at the time of demolition have the right to return. Rent increases do occur, but usually of moderate scale. This means that housing standards are improved without displacing the often poor and/or elderly inhabitants. It has to be admitted that these rebuilding activities are not meant as a social corrective, but rather intended to generate a lively, safe atmosphere in order to dilute existing social problems and maintain the global attractiveness of Tokyo.[3] Thus, these policies are not contravening the logics of entrepreneurial city politics, but they do not cause large-scale displacement of poor households.

The 1963-built Kasumigaoka complex had been on the list for demolition years before it became clear that Tokyo would host the Olympics. Due to the planned expansion of the stadium premises, it was decided not to rebuild it. Instead, tenants were offered housing in other public complexes. While this might lead to disadvantages, at least they were not left to their own devices. Another public housing complex mentioned in the context of tenant displacement due to the Olympics is Aoyama Kitamachi, scheduled for completion in early 2020.[4] Here the total amount of social housing will decrease by about 300 units from its previous form. However, the renewal project had been designed by TMG already in 2006 with the aim to adjust the social composition of the area to the wealthy neighborhoods surrounding the complex, and thus has no causal relationship to hosting the 2020 Games. On the whole, there is only scant evidence that the Olympics have directly led to displacements of tenants from public housing in Tokyo.

Gentrification Tokyo-style

As mentioned above, the volume of construction activities has soared in Tokyo following the selection in 2013, leading to voices complaining about the destruction of traditional neighborhoods. However, many such projects are carried out in easy-to-access locations such as the vicinity of local train stations far away from the sports venues of the Olympics. In most of these cases as well, planning procedures started before 2013, meaning that the Olympics may have accelerated the pace of neighborhood transformation but not initiated the renewal projects.

Apart from this, the number of housing units created by urban redevelopment projects located on industrial wasteland or newly reclaimed land at Tokyo's waterfront by far outnumbers those associated with the complete demolition of neighborhoods. In Japan, property rights on land are spatially fragmented and highly protected, requiring lengthy negotiations which leads many corporate developers to divert their energy to unused tracts of land provided by the TMG or other public actors. Such upgrading of central urban districts by new, stylish housing complexes on abandoned sites is common in many other parts of the world as well and is known by the term "new-build gentrification."

In this way, numbers of tenants directly displaced from privately rented apartments are kept comparatively low in Tokyo. In the long run, however, new-build gentrification causes displacement of lower-income groups as well, either by stimulating an increase in real estate prices of the surrounding area or by altering the socio-cultural ambience of the district, thus alienating many of the established residents from their neighborhood.[5] There are indications that such is the case in the area dealt with in the following section.

The Olympic Village and its surroundings: a redevelopment hotspot

The Olympic Village is a typical – albeit somewhat over-dimensional – case of new-build gentrification. It is constructed on a formerly unused 13.4-hectare area at the southwestern tip of Harumi Island in the innermost part of the waterfront area (see Figure 10.2). The complex is thus located at the intersection between the so-called "Heritage Zone" on the mainland and the "Tokyo Bay Zone," the way the Olympic competition sites have been named. The project includes, among other facilities, 21 residential buildings ranging from 14 to 18 stories, which will accommodate the 17,000 athletes and guests. A Bus Rapid Transit (BRT) system is intended to connect athletes (and eventually commuters, the post-Olympic future residents) with the mainland. Yet due to delays in construction, there are strong doubts whether this sole public transport connection with the city center will be ready for use in 2020. After the Games, the building consortium, which includes almost all big developers of the country, will add two 50-story buildings to the complex, increasing the number of apartments

Figure 10.2 The Olympic Village, under construction in 2019.
Source: © Barbara Holthus.

ready for sale or rent to 5,650 units. Since this would be equal to about 30% of the annual supply of new apartments in Tokyo, there are fears that there will not be enough interested residents to move in.[6]

The real estate market of the surrounding area, that is, the islands of Tsukuda (including the districts of Tsukishima and Kachidoki) and Harumi, all part of Chuo Ward, has not been left unaffected by the construction of the Olympic Village and its central location between the two venue zones. Since 2013, land prices rose much faster here than in any other area of Tokyo. Again, however, the Olympics have only accelerated a trend that had started earlier. The population on the two islands jumped from 42,096 in 2005 to 57,551 in 2013 and 74,222 in 2019. Most of the increase was due to the completion of large condominium complexes on hitherto unused land. Nevertheless, social upgrading as defined by a disproportionate rise in the proportion of residents in higher professions can be recognized in several pre-existing neighborhoods of the area as well, suggesting gradual – and moderate – displacement of poor citizens or average earners by a wealthier clientele.

Thus, Tokyo is not a tenants' paradise. Compared to other global cities, however, direct forms of residential displacement are not very common, and even hosting the 2020 Summer Olympic Games obviously has not brought change to this situation. Urban inequality in Tokyo rather manifests itself in the increasing wealth gap between inner- and outer-Tokyo due to the disproportionate influx of upper-middle class residents into the central wards, including the waterfront area.

Notes

1 http://thediplomat.com/2013/09/will-the-2020-olympics-really-help-tokyo/.
2 All citations in this paragraph were taken from: Harvey, David. 1989. "From managerialism to entrepreneurialism: The transformation in urban governance in late capitalism." *Geografiska Annaler. Series B, Human Geography* 71(1): 3–17.
3 Lützeler, Ralph. 2011. "Left behind in the global city: Spaces and places of ageing and shrinking in the Tokyo metropolitan area." In Coulmas, Florian, Ralph Lützeler (eds). *Imploding populations in Japan and Germany – a comparison.* Leiden, Boston: Brill: 473–491.
4 Mori, Chikako. 2017. "Social housing and urban renewal in Tokyo: From postwar reconstruction to the 2020 Olympic Games." In Watt, Paul, Peer Smets (eds). *Social housing and urban renewal: A cross-national perspective.* Bingley: Emerald: 277–309.
5 Lützeler, Ralph. 2008. "Population increase and 'new-build gentrification' in central Tokyo." *Erdkunde* 62(4): 287–299.
6 https://resources.realestate.co.jp.

11 Ho(s)t city

Tokyo's fight against the summer heat

Jan Lukas Kuhn

Anyone who has experienced the scorching heat and humidity of a Tokyo summer knows that without air conditioning everyday life would collapse. The average temperature in July and August rises over 30 degree Celsius in central Tokyo, the humidity reaches 70%. In July 2018, the highest temperature in Japan on record was measured close to Tokyo at 41.1 degrees. That summer a heat wave caused over 100 deaths by heatstroke and over 70,000 hospitalizations. Worries for the Olympic summer are not farfetched. Yet the original concept paper of the Japanese Olympic Committee claimed that during the timeframe from July to August "the mild weather is ideal for athletes to display their skills the best way possible." Olympic test runs in 2019 have shown the effects of the extreme heat: high water temperatures leading to an explosion of e-coli bacteria in Tokyo Bay, Odaiba and triathlon runs shortened.

There is already a host of protective equipment against Japan's summer heat in everyday life: parasols, cooling pads, and air conditioning are as characteristic of the Japanese summer as fireworks and watermelons. Hand-held electric fans started to be the rage in 2019. The Cool Biz Campaign, started by the Ministry of Environment in 2005, encourages limited use of air conditioning and a liberal dress code adjusted to the summer heat. But these measures are hardly enough to protect athletes, volunteers, and foreign visitors, let alone the Japanese populace. Some countermeasures for the Games include water-sprinkling technology and tents to cover the entrance areas of Olympic sites. For the marathon, despite heat-mitigating strategies such as special pavement, planting trees, and changing the start time, after heat issues at the Doha World Athletics Championships, the IOC moved it to the northern city of Sapporo.

In further need for countermeasures, other official suggestions have included pushing clocks back by two hours by introducing "summer time," asking stores to open their doors to cool down the area, and parasol hats for volunteers, all of which caused dismissal and ridicule, especially on social media. As extreme weather patterns continue to plague Japan, and the world for that matter, Tokyo's fight to control the heat continues. The possibility of other extreme weather, like a typhoon, would yet be another issue officials have to tackle.

12 Tokyo's architecture and urban structure

Change in an ever-changing city

Florian Purkarthofer

Shifts in urban transformation

The severe impact of Olympic Games on the urban structure of host cities is evident in many cases. Newly developed areas, stadiums, residential buildings and infrastructure projects shape the city and residents' lives even years after the Games. While the memory of the Tokyo Olympics in 1964 is still retained and the urban legacy dissolved over the years into the fabric of the city, the expectations of the 2020 Olympics' impact on space and architecture in Tokyo are oscillating between dream and nightmare. The only thing that can be taken for granted is that Tokyo is changing.

Tokyo with its fast-changing nature exhibits a particularly fluid urban fabric and significant shifts in its urban transformation. As anthropologist Jinnai Hidenobu points out in his spatial anthropology, Tokyo is structured by a "layered arrangement of history and culture, that forms the very basis of the city's life."[1] Hence, former social, legal, and spatial layers continue to affect contemporary urban changes, as well as rules, norms and discourses, albeit intangible or hidden. To explore these structures and mechanics behind the physical structures and changes, this chapter will briefly trace the historical foundations of modern Tokyo and then explore the city through the eyes of city planners.

Changing Tokyo: a continuity throughout history

Tokyo is quite young compared to other Japanese or even European cities – it celebrated its 150th anniversary in 2018. But the starting point of the urban aggregation can be antedated to the establishing of the Tokugawa Shogunate in 1603, which initiated a massive process of urbanization in Edo, the predecessor of Tokyo. In contrast to planned capitals like Nara or Kyoto, no Chinese-influenced grid masterplan had been enforced.

Edo became Tokyo in 1868, and in the following years transitioned from a feudal center to a modern nation's capital. Massive population growth and industrialization lead to rapid urbanization. This development was interrupted twice, in 1923 by the Great Kanto Earthquake, which caused fires that destroyed most of the eastern part of the city, and the air raids at the end of World War II that again razed the eastern low city (*shitamachi*) to the ground. For urban planners, such massive destructions are often an opportunity to build up from scratch. But while the buildings had burned down, ownership of plots and the social cohesion of neighborhoods remained.

This resulted in unorganized human-scale reconstruction in the aftermath of these catastrophic events. This pattern is called "scrap and build" and means replacing structures after 25 years instead of refurbishing them. It is one of the most basic modes of change, structuring the city until today. In other words, buildings are erected to be demolished in a foreseeable future, and this influences the planning horizon, design, and choice of materials. One consequence is a heterogeneous process of construction and destruction, which gives leeway to react to external changes – a helpful feature in times of destruction and still in use today.

After the war the Tokyo Metropolitan Government (TMG) introduced master plans and laws, which included rudimentary zoning, infrastructure, and developments, but they did not enforce their prompt execution. Since the late 1950s, rapid economic growth propelled an immense urban sprawl along the commuter train lines. The 1964 Tokyo Olympics symbolized these changes of the postwar high-growth era, even though most venues were built on former military lands and therefore not really cutting into the urban fabric. Showpiece projects like the Shinkansen bullet train and the elevated Tokyo Metropolitan Expressway were generally necessary, and not solely built for the Olympics. In fact, these infrastructure projects and the Olympics are part of a phenomenon that occurred due to regained economic strength and national self-esteem, forming a political narrative of "reconstruction" and a "bright future."

An architect's summary of 20th-century building practices in Japan reads: "With some exceptions, housing in Japan [especially Tokyo] happens on its own, from the bottom up. The essential rules are about the city and they are defined with a light touch."[2] It is a combination of the "scrap and build" mode of architecture and the "layered arrangements" that pervade urban space. Altogether, the outcome of the process of destructive events (fires, earthquakes, war) and infinite small changes is Tokyo: an urban conglomerate that emerged through numerous distinct (private) actions along inconspicuous rules of zoning, disaster prevention and inheritance tax. Yet, when land prices and construction costs fell after the bursting of the real estate bubble in the early 1990s and new policies in favor of "privatization and deregulation"[3] passed the parliament, corporate developers adopted a new business strategy based on buying up small plots to erect multiuse skyscrapers, or "super-blocks." This mode of corporate-scale redevelopment stands in sharp contrast to the scrap and build mode: It takes years to plan and build those concrete towers, so they are not easy to dismantle, and they produce commodified, homogenous city space instead of human-scale heterogeneity.

Acceleration and escapism: the urban impact and spectacle of Tokyo 2020

"To understand Tokyo's bids for the Olympic Games [the unsuccessful 2016 bid and the successful 2020 bid] means to acknowledge the power of real estate developers, [their adjunct construction companies and estate agents] and their practices," a young city planner voiced at a gathering of planning professionals serenely. "It might be sports, spectacle, or a political show for us, but for the developers it is serious big business," one of his colleagues continued.

The role of real estate developers becomes clear by focusing on the Olympic Village, branded under the name "Harumi Flag" for the domestic housing market. The land, constructed through land fillings in Tokyo Bay dating back to the 1930s, was slated to host the International Exposition and Tokyo's first Olympics, both scheduled for 1940 yet cancelled because of World War II. The TMG paid for the construction of residential buildings to host the 17,000 athletes of the 2020 Olympic and Paralympic Games, but already sold the property back again to the main developers for a sixth of its market value. For them, the construction of the super-block architecture as well as the redistribution after the Games promises to be a profitable investment. New apartment blocks at the waterfront are also spreading alongside the Olympic Village. At some sites in the eastern low city, they are actively replacing small scale structures that were often considered "the real Tokyo." The 2020 Olympic Games are fueling and accelerating the construction activities that lead to the vanishing of the old city feel. One such example is the relocation of the Tsukiji fish market, the world's largest (see Figure 12.1).

Former Vice-Governor of Tokyo Aoyama Yasushi prefers to envision the positive effects of "urban development," "improved infrastructure," and a "change of civic life" for a "matured society of sports and leisure."[4] Contrary to this optimistic perspective, more sinister or pessimistic views regarding the outcome exist as well: "Maybe it is a deception to give people hope and something to talk and think about, but social and

Figure 12.1 Redevelopment of former Tsukiji fish market into Olympic transport hub, 2019.

Source: © Isaac Gagné.

economic problems won't be solved by the Olympic Games. What can you do?" commented an architecture consultant. After two decades of economic recession in the 1990s–2000s, the catastrophic earthquake, tsunami and nuclear incident of March 2011, and the reality of a shrinking and aging population, the political instrumentalization of the Olympic Games is comprehensible. Besides a positively tuned bureaucracy, this buoyant outlook might also explain why many unrelated undertakings, such as infrastructure developments, reconstruction measures, and urban improvements, are scheduled to be finished in 2020. It is "a sunny spot in a not so bright future," said a young bureaucrat as a summary of his view that the 2020 Olympics are more escapism than eudaimonia.

Whose Games? Whose city? The urge for legacy

The critical question of "whose Games the Tokyo Olympics are" is not easy to answer, but it is quite simple in terms of the brick-and-mortar aspects: The construction and real estate businesses sack the profits, while the national and metropolitan governments harvest a political success story and positive media coverage, resulting in increased international tourism. In contrast, those who live and work in Tokyo are requested to comply and work around this event at their own sacrifice.

This leads us to the second important question regarding the critical assessment of the urban legacy that prevails long after the Games have left for the next host city, Paris 2024: Whose city is Tokyo? The Japan Association of City Planners in 2015 proposed seven recommendations for a balanced post-Olympics legacy, voicing the concerns of inhabitants. They advocate for ecological visions and standards, a sustainable urban landscape, open and human-centered waterfront development, walkable living environments, barrier-free infrastructure, flexible, community-centered institutions, and re-naturalization.[5] While progress can be seen regarding some aspects such as barrier-free(er) public transport and efforts to strengthen communities based on urban development (*machizukuri*), other proposals concerning sustainability and ecological visions are clearly contradicted by corporate interests and the governmental plans to increase international mass tourism.

Undoubtedly, the ever-changing character of Tokyo is not jeopardized by the 2020 Olympics and Paralympics; it is just another event that contributes momentum to the process. And yet, as revealed above, the open question is which changes, in which mode, to what amount, by whom are shaping the next stratum of Tokyo, and these decisions are not finalized but similarly contested. In other words: "The rulebook that controls Tokyo is flexible. The future vision of the city is outlined but not planned in detail."[6] This flexibility is the city's biggest strength when facing future challenges, but if small-scale change is hamstringed by a preponderance of corporate interests, it also constitutes a vulnerability for the urban organism that is Tokyo.

Notes

1 Jinnai, Hidenobu. 1995. *Tokyo: A spatial anthropology*. Berkeley: University of California Press: 220.
2 See Galloway, William, et al., 2017. "What rules make (Tokyo's secret code)." In Mundle, Kent (ed.), *House us*. Winnipeg: OCDI Press: 179–186.
3 Tsukamoto, Yoshiharu, Jorge Almazán. 2006. "Scrap and build: Alternatives to the corporate redevelopment of Tokyo." *MONU – Magazine on Urbanism* 4: 6–9.
4 Aoyama Yasushi. 2014. "Olympic cities. Spatial planning challenges for the 2020 Tokyo Olympics." *The Japanese Journal of Real Estate Sciences* 28: 42–48.
5 Nihon Toshi Keikakuka Kyōkai [Japan society of urban and regional planners]. 2015. *2020nen Tōkyō Orinpikku pararinpikku – mirai e no regashī to suru tame no nanatsu no teigen* [2020 Tokyo Olympics and Paralympics]. Tokyo: Nihon Toshi Keikakuka Kyōkai.
6 Galloway et al. 2017: 185.

13 Success story

The 1964 Tokyo Olympics

Torsten Weber

There is little doubt that the 1964 Olympics were a huge success for Japan and Tokyo. To make travel easy for visitors, spectators, and athletes and to display Japan's cutting-edge technology, billions of yen were spent to construct city highways, the Shinkansen, and the Monorail. The latter linked Tokyo's international airport Haneda to the city, and after completion in September 1964 many Tokyoites are said to have taken the Monorail just for the experience (see Figure 13.1). New sports facilities were built, among them the Yoyogi National Gymnasium designed by Kenzo Tange and the Olympic Park in Komazawa, originally planned for the abandoned 1940 Olympics. Tokyoites still use them today as popular sports and recreation facilities. The landmark-building Nippon Budokan was especially built to host the Olympic newcomer sport of judo. Needless to say, Japanese athletes won three out of four gold medals in that sport.

In total, Japanese athletes won 16 gold medals, earning the Japanese team a record third rank in the medal table. Famously, Japan's legendary women's volleyball team – nicknamed *Tōyō no majo* (Oriental witches) – beat the Soviet Union in the final match of the tournament to clinch the title of Olympic champions. The opening day of the Games, October 10, became a public holiday (Health and Sports Day) in 1966, together with the reinstallation of National Foundation Day, which had been abolished by the Occupation Forces after World War II. The Olympics also created a boom in consumerism: sales numbers of televisions peaked, hyped by the first live Olympic broadcast via satellite and the introduction of color TVs.

Historian Christian Tagsold writes that the 1964 Tokyo Olympics reaffirmed Japanese citizens' pride in the country's postwar achievements and reinforced its identity as a modern and successful nation that had stepped out of the dark shadows of the past and regained respect from the international community. And Tokyo, in the words of journalist Robert Whiting, was "transformed from a struggling third-world capital into a shiny international metropolis." This success story is undisputed and has been told many times. Yet, native Tokyoites will also remind you of the annoyances of toxic pollution, deafening noise, and horrendous smell in their city caused by the increase in traffic and the poor sewage system as well as of environmental destruction and forced relocations that enabled the frantic pre-Games construction rush.

Figure 13.1 Linking the past with the future, at Haneda airport, 2017.

Source: © Torsten Weber.

14 San'ya 2020

From building to hosting the Tokyo Olympics

Hanno Jentzsch

Our small volunteer group gathered in the lobby of the Juyoh Hotel, a tall building in the center of San'ya, Tokyo's infamous day laborer quarter. Buzzing with positive energy, the hotel manager handed out plastic bags and gloves, and we set out on our mission to clean up the streets around the hotel. An hour later, we had collected some regular trash and countless empty beer cans and small sake containers, the remains of an active public drinking scene. The hotel manager's weekly clean-up effort illustrates the ongoing transformation of San'ya, where the onset of international tourism has come to intersect with the decline of the day laborer quarter. Both the 1964 Olympics and Tokyo 2020 are important milestones in this process.

San'ya is a small district spanning the northern part of Taito Ward and a small corner of Arakawa Ward in northern Tokyo. In many ways, it has been the antithesis to the image that Tokyo seeks to communicate to the world – modern, affluent, clean, and safe. In the postwar era, it became one of the three major day laborer quarters (*doya-gai*) in Japan. The *doya-gai* emerged from San'ya's long history as a place for men who "had fallen through the cracks of society and family."[1] Until the early 20th century, the area hosted an execution ground. The big intersection cutting through San'ya is still called Namidabashi, the "bridge of tears," where delinquents would bid farewell to their loved ones. Already before World War II, San'ya was known for cheap lodging and prostitution. Immediately after the war, it became a designated barrack zone, and eventually home to a growing number of men who sought work in San'ya's open-air day labor market (*yoseba*). They lived crammed in cheap and simple hostels, called *doya*. Around the 1964 Tokyo Olympics, more than 220 *doya* hosted more than 15,000 day laborers. As the flexible labor reserve of the mushrooming Japanese construction industry, these men played a crucial, but often forgotten role in building the facilities for the 1964 Games, and the booming city around it. Meanwhile, San'ya itself built its reputation of being a rowdy, *yakuza*-infested, and politically explosive place.[2] Many *doya* are still in business today. But with Tokyo 2020 on the horizon, San'ya has taken on a strikingly different role. Offering both cheap accommodation and easy access, the district will host thousands of visitors from all around the world during the global mega-event. However, the transformation from sheltering day laborers to welcoming visitors for the 2020 Games has not been a smooth process.

From day labor to social welfare

San'ya today is not what it used to be in the postwar era. The number of day laborers has steadily declined due to the aging of the almost exclusively male workers, and a lack of fresh blood. In addition, since the burst of the economic bubble in the late 1980s, getting work off the streets in the construction sector – the main industry using day labor in Japan – has become harder and harder. Moreover, the industry increasingly relies on foreign workers for cheap and flexible labor. Recent reforms have accelerated this trend. Not least, the need for the *yoseba* as a physical space for brokering day labor has declined, since short-term gigs are now mostly solicited online. Compared to the postwar period, day laborers thus can and do live anywhere.

Even though the *yoseba* itself has almost disappeared, the day laborer history still shapes everyday life in San'ya. Around 3,800 people live in approximately 150 *doya*, the large majority of them former day laborers on social welfare.[3] The area has turned from a day laborer quarter into a welfare quarter, says Niiro Sho, a photographer who worked in San'ya for years. And due to aging, alcoholism, and frequent cases of mental illness, it is now further changing into an "elderly care" quarter. According to data gathered by the welfare department of Taito Ward, most *doya* residents want to stay in San'ya – it has become the home for those who have nowhere else to go. The Tokyo Metropolitan Government provides limited opportunities for publicly funded short-term labor, and as most *doya* residents by now can work only occasionally, or not at all,[4] groups of men can be seen in the daytime gathering, drinking, and chatting in the streets.

Now and then, those who cannot afford a room in one of the *doya* have to sleep rough – some only for a few days until the next paycheck or welfare payment arrives, others for longer periods of time. A small park off the main road has long been a site for the occasionally or permanently homeless. Other men camp in a shopping street on the other side of the main road. Until recently, this shopping street had a roof and was called Iroha Arcade. The arcade was one of the social centers of day-laboring life in San'ya, close to the building of the main welfare organization in the area, and a dry place for gathering, drinking, and sleeping. The roof was taken down in early 2018 on initiative of the shop owners and the Taito Ward government. The ward argues there were security concerns – who would have taken responsibility if the worn-out roof had buried the campers underneath it? A man drinking in the streets assumes the roof came down as a beautification effort for Tokyo 2020. Either way, people continue to sleep rough in the former arcade, some of them in tents.

From *doya-gai* to backpacker-*gai*

The Juyoh Hotel represents the other major trend that has been transforming San'ya: international tourism. In the early 2000s, some *doya* owners began to open their establishments for businessmen, job seekers, and travelers on a tight budget, as a reaction to the decreasing number of day laborers. The inflow of tourists was fueled by another major sports event: the 2002 Soccer World Cup in Japan and Korea. And it has not stopped there. San'ya is close to the major tourist sites in Asakusa, and easily accessible via Minami-Senju Station. Rooms are cheap. Even today, one can spend a night for less than \$30. Thus, especially younger travelers and backpackers have been drawn to the area. Many *doya* have renovated some or all rooms to receive domestic and international tourists. This did not happen on private initiative alone. The Taito Ward government has been supporting the modernization of (former) *doya* into tourist facilities with a subsidy program since the early 2000s.[5] New hotels have also opened in and around the neighborhood, some of them directly appealing to international visitors. Groups of foreign tourists wandering around the narrow streets in search for their place to stay have become a common sight in San'ya.

With a record number of international visitors expected, the 2020 Olympics mark another milestone in this development – and thus a particularly pronounced clash between the old San'ya and its emerging new role. Apart from the Taito Ward government, many private initiatives are now engaged in reinventing "San'ya 2020" as an open, clean neighborhood, in which the day laborer history might become merely a commodifiable backstory. Some hotels in the area already use San'ya's rowdy image for advertising. Yet, for the remaining *doya* residents, this backstory is still their everyday life. If one takes the recent deconstruction of the Iroha Arcade as a symbolic indicator, the transformation of the area is not without tensions. How will the efforts of those who seek to reinvent the area as a site for modern hospitality affect those who have long been relying on San'ya's unique social infrastructure, geared toward the needs of day laborers, outcasts, and welfare recipients? Indeed, some international visitors are shocked about the public drinking and the run-down outward appearance of San'ya, says the manager of the Juyoh Hotel.

Obviously, many local entrepreneurs, residents, and not least the police would not mind if the actual remains of San'ya's "backstory" would conveniently disappear. But at the same time, not everyone in San'ya wants to get rid of the day laborers and welfare recipients. Many of the older *doya* are neither willing nor suited to welcome foreign guests, and in fact anybody else other than male (former) day laborers. The rates of such traditional *doya* seem to be independent from the tourist development. As Niiro explains, these establishments have little incentive to raise prices. Their rates correspond to the monthly welfare payments. The welfare recipients thus form a stable source of publicly subsidized income. San'ya also hosts a large number of welfare organizations. Activists are eager to preserve the area as a place of refuge for aging welfare recipients, alcoholics, and homeless.

Adding to the complexity, the political authorities at the ward level and the metropolitan government take an ambiguous stance toward the redevelopment of San'ya. This is because the area has long served as a convenient place to concentrate, and thereby contain, urban poverty, homelessness, public drinking, and – especially in the early days – the radical political activism of the day laborers. Thus, the *doya-gai* served a practical purpose not only for its long-term residents, but also for the state, says Niiro. Taito Ward's welfare department acknowledges that most (former) day laborers have nowhere else to go; at the same time, authorities have also been eager to move homeless persons into the social welfare system in recent years. While the number of homeless persons in Japan has declined, activists criticize this development as hiding poverty instead of alleviating it. Relocation efforts of homeless are expected to increase in the context of the 2020 Olympics, in order to remove visible poverty from the touristic landmarks. San'ya with its unique social infrastructure is one of the potential places to receive relocated homeless. The upcoming Olympics are thus a focal point of the diverging interests shaping San'ya's transformation: the public and private promotion of a new, touristic San'ya, the needs of the *doya* residents, and the ongoing interest of public authorities to control, if not to hide social problems in a small, confined space.

Diversifying San'ya

This complex constellation of actors and interests is by no means new – in contrast to other Japanese day-laborer quarters, the day-laboring world and "normal" residents have long been coexisting in San'ya. The manager of the Juyoh Hotel thus believes that the area needs to embrace diversification to ease the friction associated with its transformation. For her, this means ensuring that there is a place for all the social elements that make up San'ya today. Embodying this idea, she manages three establishments in San'ya: The Juyoh Hotel, which is explicitly geared towards international guests, a "hybrid" hostel for tourists on a tight budget, day laborers and welfare recipients, and an establishment exclusively for the most troubled members of San'ya's society, including those who suffer from mental illnesses. In addition, building upon her independent research on the challenges of *doya* residents, she also runs an NPO that aims to support the local welfare recipients. In the same spirit of ensuring the peaceful coexistence in the changing neighborhood, she initiated her weekly neighborhood clean-up group. Besides picking up trash, the volunteer group also checks in with the men in the streets, and exchanges information or friendly salutations. Most members of the group have a history of living in San'ya or still reside in the area. After every tour, they meet in the San'ya Café, a small eatery in the Juyoh lobby. The manager opened the café in 2018 as part of her civic engagement. It is supposed to be a place where *doya* residents and international hotel guests have a chance to get to know each other – the physical manifestation of her vision of "San'ya 2020."

Notes

1 Fowler, Edward. 1998. *Sanya blues: Laboring life in contemporary Tokyo.* Ithaca: Cornell University Press: 15.
2 For details on San'ya's history and the postwar situation of day laborers, see e.g. ibid; Gill, Tom. 1994. "Sanya Street Life under the Heisei Recession." *Japan Quarterly* 41(3): 270–286.
3 Interview, Jōhoko Welfare Centre, January 2020.
4 Interview, Taito Ward Welfare Department, March 2019.
5 Ibid.

15 Baseball/softball

One more homer for Japan

Wolfram Manzenreiter

Baseball first appeared at the Olympics in St. Louis in 1904. It became an official part of the program in 1992, only to become the second sport voted out of the program by the IOC in 2005, after Polo in the 1930s.

Finding baseball among the five new sports for Tokyo 2020 was highly predictable. Baseball was first introduced to Japan in 1872 and quickly developed a fan base among students and industrial workers. Backed up by mass media, it soon turned into Japan's de facto national sport. By the 1920s, high school championships, university league games, and workers' tournaments drew large audiences to the ballparks. Until today the Kōshien high school tournament of champions from all 47 prefectures is *the* highlight of Japan's annual sport calendar and a secular ritual celebrating the virtues of youth – and the end of summer.

Professional baseball started in 1934. Nowadays it's shown virtually daily on TV during the season starting in April. Six teams each play in the Central and the Pacific League to qualify for the all-decisive Japan Series in October. Yomiuri Giants and Hanshin Tigers are the most popular teams representing the epic antagonism of East and West Japan.

Tokyo 2020 stars two events of men's baseball and women's softball. Differences between the sibling sports are negligible, with softball using a smaller playing field, shorter bats, a lighter ball, and a distinctively different throwing technique. The host nation's athletes are set for both events, and the remaining five teams of each event are decided at continental qualifiers. The World Baseball Softball Confederation changed some rules for the Olympic event to shorten games and keep audiences in suspense about the result of the three-stage double-elimination format. Group winners from the second knock-off round will play for gold, and runners-up compete for bronze. Japan is one serious contender for the gold medal. The country currently leads the men's baseball world rankings and women are runners-up in softball.

Rule changes also made it possible that for the first time both sports can be staged at the same venue. Most games will be hosted by the Yokohama Baseball Stadium. However, one match in baseball and six in softball are played at the Fukushima Azuma Stadium, close-by to the area hit hardest by the March 2011 triple disaster.

16 Outdoor sports in the periphery

Far from the compact games

Daniel Kremers

In their bid for the 32nd Olympiad the Tokyo Organising Committee of the Olympic and Paralympic Games (TOCOG) promised to hold "compact Games in the heart of the city."[1] With 28 of the 33 competition venues within eight kilometers of the Olympic and Paralympic Village, Tokyo 2020 aimed at becoming one of the most compact Games ever held. After Tokyo won the bid in the final round against Madrid and Istanbul, however, it became clear that not all that was promised could be delivered. While most of the events are still concentrated within the 23 districts of Tokyo, venues for several disciplines were relocated, while sites for sports that will have their Olympic debut in 2020 had to be sought outside of Tokyo, making the 2020 Games actually the most regionally dispersed in Olympic history, and rural municipalities suddenly find themselves hosting the Olympic and Paralympic mega-events.

Rural municipalities in Japan are faced with economic decline, aging, and shrinking populations – much more than urban centers like Tokyo or Osaka. In 2015, a government study identified 15,568 rural hamlets with over 50% of the population above the age of 65. Far from being a cure for all, hosting sport events and promoting athletic activities in general is a common strategy to increase the attractiveness of a locality for residents and employers, and a small but increasing number of local communities are focusing on outdoor and adventure sports to attract young people. The Tokyo 2020 Olympic and Paralympic Games thus offer a chance to look closer at urban-rural relations in Japan.

Finding suitable locations

Tokyo is one of the most densely populated places on earth. This makes it extremely challenging to find available space suitable for building sport infrastructures of Olympic dimensions, especially when it comes to outdoor sports. Tokyo's bid introduced two combined concepts. Renovating and reusing 1964 facilities in a so-called "Heritage Zone" and building new facilities on reclaimed land in the "Tokyo Bay Zone." However, together with the dismantling and rebuilding of the national stadium in central Tokyo, building new and mostly temporary facilities blew cost calculations out of proportion, and was hard to reconcile with Tokyo's other goal of creating social and environmental sustainability legacies.

With the aim of saving $1 billion, the two Inner City Zones were stretched from a circle of eight kilometers to two ovals of more than 50 kilometers in length, spanning from Musashino Forest Sport Plaza in the west to Makuhari Messe in Chiba Prefecture to the east. Additionally, several sports and disciplines where moved further away – ten venues in the Olympics and 19 venues in the Paralympics. Basketball was moved to Saitama Super Arena, Fencing, Taekwondo, and Wrestling were moved from their central location next to the Olympic Village out to Makuhari in Chiba prefecture, and sailing was moved from Tokyo Bay to Enoshima Yacht Harbor in Kanagawa prefecture, 60 kilometers to the south of central Tokyo.

The greatest changes affected cycling. In April 2015 plans surfaced to move track cycling, mountain biking and BMX from Ariake and Sea Forest Park in Tokyo Bay to the Japan Cycle Sports Center (CSC), a theme park in the city of Izu, 130 kilometers from Tokyo. The CSC had been established in 1965, one year after the 1964 Olympics, with the aim to promote cycling in Japan. Since 2011 it features Japan's only wooden indoor velodrome. After lengthy negotiations with the International Cycling Union (UCI), the final agreement allowed only BMX to stay in the Tokyo Bay Zone. Road races start in Western Tokyo, pass through Yamanashi Prefecture and end in Shizuoka Prefecture, while mountain biking and track cycling were moved to the CSC. With all but one of the four cycling disciplines having been moved to two separate locations in Shizuoka Prefecture, it makes them the most distant events of any Olympic and Paralympic Games in history.

Another outdoor sport, surfing will make its Olympic debut in 2020. Japan has an abundance of surfing beaches, but with none within the Tokyo metropolis, a rural solution had to be found as well. The organizers opted for Ichinomiya in Chiba prefecture, roughly 90 kilometers to the East of central Tokyo, whose beaches are a popular destination for surfers from all over Japan.

Turf and Surf in Izu and Ichinomiya

Izu City is used to international cycling events at the CSC, but nothing like the Olympic Games. The town hall's business bureau has set up a team to prepare for the event. The major concern is accommodation capacity for media personnel and spectators, who will compete for rooms and beds with ordinary summer season visitors. A local NPO has set up bike rental stations and bike racks at points of interest, to boost cycling tourism before and after the Games. While Izu Velodrome is a popular destination for track cyclists, and the local mountain bike course hosts the annual CSC-Classic cross-country race, the CSC was not overly successful in its mission to promote cycling.

CSC is doing little in terms of destination management. Its website is old, with links to "Izu-Cycle-Mecca" not working at all. The CSC and track cycling in Japan in general are dominated by *keirin*, a race format popular for sport betting, and the CSC's contribution to other disciplines is rather small. BMX is very popular in Japan, but mostly due to its fashionable urban image mainly transported through US popular culture, while road cycling owes much of its popularity to the Tour de France and manga comics like *Yowamushi Pedal*. Copying the French original, the rural city of Iida in Nagano prefecture attracts visitors by annually hosting the Tour de Japon. Sales of mountain bikes boomed in the 1990s, but the sport did not gain wider acceptance. Though abundant in forests and mountains, Japan lacks courses and trails due to a fine-grained and complicated ownership of land without right-of-way rules, an extreme concern for safety, and too little free time to spend building trails, among other challenges.[2] Opaque traffic rules, a lack of bicycle lanes and the ban of bicycles from public transport discourage many Japanese from cycling, even on paved roads. This corresponds to recent findings of a Chiba University study revealing that 70% of Japan's elementary school children do not even play outside, both in urban as well as rural areas.[3] Against these odds it is doubtful that the 2020 Olympic and Paralympic events at CSC can do much to promote cycling in all its variety in Japan, and if the CSC does not change its focus on *keirin*, it will also do little to promote the rural region of Izu through cycling as an outdoor activity.

Ichinomiya in Chiba prefecture came into the spotlight of the 2020 Games for hosting the Olympic debut of surfing. Already now the town is benefitting from the sport. Though Ichinomiya is small with a population of only 12,000, well below the Japanese average of 77,000, each year 600,000 surfers visit the local beaches. Families and young adults moved here to be close to the surf. The local elementary school is cramped with surfer kids. The town even built housing with facilities specially catering to surfers such as outside showers.[4] Hosting the Olympics will thus build on and expand a strategy that has already proved successful. The chances that the 2020 Games will leave a sustainable legacy in Ichinomiya are thus very high.

Beyond 2020: outdoor sports as drivers for rural revitalization in Japan

With approximately 3,000 kilometers of coastline facing the Pacific Ocean, Japan has an abundance of beaches that are frequented by surfers. Closest to Tokyo are the beaches of Kamakura and Enoshima to the south, and Chiba's Katsu'ura and Ichinomiya to the east. Local hotels and lodges especially cater to surfers, surfing schools make the sport attractive and accessible for beginners, and boards can be rented at many places. Another reason that surfing is so popular in Japan is certainly the positive image of Hawai'i as one of the most popular tourist destinations among Japanese. A major Japanese car manufacturer recently launched an edition of a popular minivan that is especially trimmed to the needs of surfers. Thus, surfing is a major outdoor sport in Japan and already contributing to the attractiveness of coastal areas. I talked with my neighbors in suburban Tokyo, a couple with a young daughter, who are avid surfers. Though they regularly drive their pick-up truck to Kamakura for surfing, they consider the distance to Ichinomiya quite far. Nonetheless, they have applied for tickets to see the Olympic competitions there.

Mountain biking on the other hand has had it more difficult than surfing, mainly due to access to forests and mountains in Japan. During the first wave of the sport's popularity in the early 1990s conflicts quickly ensued with hikers and landowners, as mountain bikers used to flock in large groups at popular hiking spots such as Mount Takao in the west of Tokyo, where mountain bikes have been banned as a result. A couple of ski-resorts operate bike parks in summer, such as Fujimi Panorama, Fujiten, and Iwatake in Hakuba that hosted the 1998 Nagano Winter Games. More recently, local voluntary associations are utilizing mountain biking as a tool of rural revitalization, thereby improving the sport's image. Following the example of the International Mountain Bike Association (IMBA), a US-Canadian organization, these groups focus more on trail-building than athletic competition. But they are also engaged in typical Japanese community activities such as garbage collection, disaster prevention, and festival (*matsuri*) preparations. Thus, through mountain biking, they actively provide assets to the local community. The most active clubs are based in Nishitama, Minami Alps, Sanjo, Mino, Tottori, and Saga. Especially the group in Minami Alps puts a strong emphasis on motivating young people to migrate from the urban centers to the rural peripheries, so-called U- and I-turners.[5]

While some members of these groups are enthusiastic about the attention given to their sport, such as in a recent campaign by the job agency Recruit that portrayed "trail builder" as a job "helping Tokyo 2020,"[6] they are nonetheless realistic about future prospects. They will have to continue to negotiate with local governments, land owners, and other stakeholders for every meter of trail. Making the benefits of outdoor sports visible and changing the hearts and minds of the elderly population in rural Japan is not an easy task. Nonetheless, outdoor sports such as surfing and mountain biking have demonstrated tremendous potential for rural areas outside Japan. As they cannot be practiced in urban conglomerations, rural areas can foster them to attract visitors and migrants on the one hand, while making the region more attractive for residents, improving public health and well-being as well as raising the utility and value of otherwise unused land. Without locals actively promoting sports and outdoor activities, however, there will be no long-lasting positive effects of rurally hosted mega-events.

Originally, the main argument for having compact Games was that the Olympic and Paralympics Games are an event for athletes, not for spectators. Bringing athletes from all over the world together in one Olympic Village is considered a core element of the Games. Having competitions away from the Village thus runs the risk of excluding groups from the Olympic experience. Furthermore, as Tokyo won the bid on the promise of compact Games, spreading out could be seen as cheating, which might encourage other cities to come up with unrealistic plans in the future. But having less compact Games may not necessarily be a bad thing. Hosting events outside of Tokyo might help bring rural areas into the spotlight, while the variety of disciplines of 2020 might help to increase the popularity of outdoor sports that carry great potential in economic and social terms but have so far been underappreciated in Japan.

Notes

1 Tokyo Organising Committee of the Olympic and Paralympic Games (TOCOG). 2012. *Discover Tomorrow Tokyo 2020.* http://tokyo2020.org/en/games/plan/data/candidate1-intro-ENFR.pdf.
2 Hirano, Yuichiro. 2016. "Mauntenbaikā ni yoru arata shinrin riyō kokoromi to kanōsei" [New challenges and possibilities of forest use by mountain bikers]. *Nichirinshi* 98: 1–10.
3 The Mainichi. May 31, 2019. "More than 70% of kids in urban, rural Japan not playing outside." https://mainichi.jp/english/articles/20190530/p2a/00m/0na/032000c.
4 NHK World. December 5, 2018. "Town hopes to ride the Tokyo 2020 wave." www3.nhk.or.jp/nhkworld/nhknewsline/backstories/tokyo2020wave/index.html.
5 Minami Arupusu Mauntenbaiku Aikōkai. www.minamialpsmtb.com/.
6 Recruit. 2019. *Sasaeru 2020 no shigoto* [Jobs that support 2020]. https://recruit-2020.tokyo/.

17 Surfing

Taken with a grain of salt

Wolfram Manzenreiter

2020 will be a big year for surfing – especially in Japan, where surfing currently recovers from a decade-long slump. Surfing sociologist Mizuno Eri estimates there are 250,000 surfers, 80% male, down from 750,000 a few years earlier. Surfing is marked as hip and fashionable, as in previous booms, when sun-tanned "hill surfers" sporting the right shabby chic cruised in cars with boards tied to their roof through Roppongi, but never close to the shoreline.

Japan never ranked high on the global travel circuit of surfers, for reasons of excess in costs and scarcity of space in the waters at popular spots. Yet the country has a shoreline of almost 30,000 kilometers, with countless beach-breaks, rivermouths, and pointbreaks. The best season to surf is summer, when an average of 15 to 20 typhoons track north over Japan and create a short-lived swell in the surrounding seas. A two-to-four-foot surf is common, but typhoons may create waves of up to 40 feet.

Making surfing Olympic was made a strategic priority for the International Surfing Association (ISA) in 1995. Since then, ISA membership increased from 32 nations to 106, reaching non-traditional surfing destinations such as Iran, Sierra Leone, and Russia. At Tokyo 2020, 20 men and 20 women will compete on shortboards. Judges will score speed, power, and flow of rides of four athletes each in 25-minute heats and decide who continues to the next round. Chances are good for Igarashi Kanoa, the youngest surfer ever to win the US National Championships at age 14 and Matsuda Shino, age 16.

Rumors had it that surfing's Olympic debut would happen in a Slater Wave pool, rather than adventuring the unpredictability of ocean tide and weather. Japan has been a forerunner in artificial waves and surf lagoons, starting with Tokyo Summerland in 1967 and Blue Wild Yokohama in 1992. Putting the contest into a pool would have set the event on an immutable schedule and facilitated comparing surfers' performances. Keeping Olympic surfing salted brings problems for TV programmers but pleases Mabuchi Masaya, mayor of Ichinomiya where the contest will be held. With the havocked Fukushima Daiichi nuclear reactors just 300 kilometers up the coast, Olympic surfing in Ichinomiya will be a powerful message to demonstrate that the waters are safe.

18 Tokyo's 1940 "Phantom Olympics" in public memory

When Japan chose war over the Olympics

Torsten Weber

Olympic memory and Japan's history problems

Ever since its defeat in 1945, Japan has been struggling to come to terms with its World War II past. Even today there is no public consensus on some key questions such as Japan's role as victim or perpetrator and the issue of war crimes vis-à-vis China and Korea. As a consequence, references to the period between 1931 and 1945 are scarce and ambiguous in Japanese public discourse.[1] Japan's Olympic memory reflects this ambiguity. Whereas mass media and official metropolitan and national organizations often forgo references to the 12th Olympic Games, scheduled to take place in Tokyo in 1940, the revisionist National Showa Memorial Museum (Showakan) in Tokyo takes a much more up-front approach.

When on September 8, 2013 Tokyo was chosen to host the 2020 Olympic Games, celebrations of the successful application and anticipation of this international mega-event quickly blended with nostalgia for the first Tokyo Games in 1964. On the same day, special issues of national newspapers announced "Tokyo Olympic decision, second time, after 56 years." The *Asahi* newspaper dedicated a full-color page to "moving moments" of 1964, while the *Nikkei* celebrated Tokyo as "the first city in Asia that will host the Games for a second time." The *Mainichi* included a special section on the "great success" of the 1964 Games: Japan's record third rank in the medal table, the start of the high-speed Shinkansen train service between Tokyo and Osaka, and the first Olympic live broadcast on color TVs. It also reminded its readers of Sakai Yoshinori, the last runner in the 1964 torch relay who lit the Olympic flame in the National Stadium. Sakai was born in Hiroshima on the day the atomic bomb was dropped. This reference to Japanese victimhood was the only reference to the war. Even the Olympic timeline on its front page neatly omitted the period between 1936 and 1948 despite the Olympic Games having been scheduled to take place in Tokyo for the first time in 1940. In the jubilant mood of September 2013, the fact that Tokyo had won the bid to host the Games for a third (1940, 1964, 2020), not second, time was simply ignored. The success story of Tokyo 1964 was immediately targeted as the sole historic focus of public Olympic remembrance.

It took the Tokyo Metropolitan Edo-Tokyo Museum less than one week to open the special exhibition "Olympics coming to Tokyo, 1964–2020" in September 2013. Exhibits included the iconic red uniform worn by the athletes during the opening ceremony, an original ticket from that ceremony, posters, and other souvenirs from 1964. While a small section addressed the forfeited Games of 1940, its accompanying explanation is revealing, stating Tokyo returned the right to host the Games "as the global conditions worsened." No word of the war, no word of Japan's invasion of China. One year later, the same museum opened a follow-up exhibition that focused even more explicitly on remembering the "glory of 1964." It explained how the Shinkansen and the 1964 Games were intertwined symbols of Japan's "democratization, economic recovery and international appeal." Original first-class seats from the Shinkansen, a tobacco box showing the train and the word "peace," and a color TV from 1963 were on display. The message was clear: peaceful and democratic Japan was back at the forefront of technological innovation and receiving global recognition. In this and similar ways, 1964 has rhetorically been linked to 2020 during the past seven years between 2013 and 2020. Yet just as revisionists ignore Japan's war responsibility, the year 1940 has largely been wiped from Japan's Olympic memory. 1940: the year of Tokyo's "Phantom Olympics."[2]

"No horses and only wood"

How did Tokyo 1940 become the "Phantom Olympics?" Everything started in 1931 when Tokyo's Municipal Assembly decided to enter the bidding process. 1940 was selected as the target year, because the Games would coincide with the mythical 2,600th anniversary of Japanese imperial reign. Tokyo's international lobbying activities began in 1932 and at the IOC's general assembly in 1935, Helsinki, Rome, and Tokyo entered the bidding race. On July 31, 1936, one day before Hitler opened the Berlin Olympics, Tokyo was selected as the host city of the 12th Olympic Games in 1940, a truly historic decision. For the first time ever, a city outside of Europe or North America was to host the Games.

Back in Japan, the preparations started immediately. A committee of city, state, and sports officials was formed to coordinate the planning. Within a year, the organizers drew up plans to construct an Olympic Park in Komazawa and even started the merchandising of souvenir products. A contest to select the official Olympic poster was held and received 2,000 submissions. The winning poster displayed an oversized portrayal of the mythical Emperor Jimmu – who according to legend ascended the Japanese throne in 660 BC – the Olympic rings, and Mount Fuji. However, it did not pass Japanese censorship authorities, which forbade portrayals of any emperor on posters and it had to be retracted in favor of other designs (see Figure 18.1). The financial burden of constructing new sports facilities and accommodations was among the biggest worries initially. Internationally, however, problems were even bigger. In 1931, Japan occupied Manchuria and founded the puppet-state of Manchukuo in 1932. Following international protests, Japan announced its withdrawal from the League of Nations in 1933 but remained committed to its participation in international organizations, including the International Olympic Committee (IOC). The outbreak of the Sino-Japanese War in July 1937, however, turned the tides. Although the Japanese military had taken the Chinese

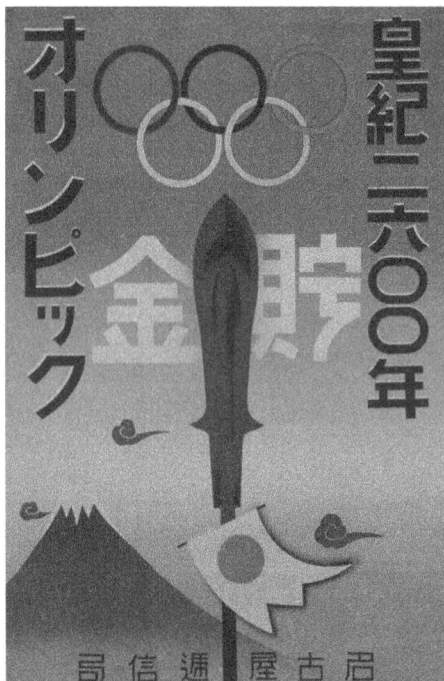

Figure 18.1 A saving campaign poster issued by Nagoya's post office featuring Olympic logo, with the words "2600th Imperial Anniversary" (*c.*1936–1938).

Source: © Advertising Museum Tokyo.

capital of Nanjing as early as December 1937, it quickly became clear that the war would not be over within weeks or months. Against this background, international pressure rose on Japan. While Japanese in Tokyo took English language classes to prepare for the international visitors and the sale of Olympic memorabilia was well under way, the Japanese Foreign Ministry received a clear message from IOC president Henri de Baillet-Latour: if Japan were not to stop its war in China, many countries were expected to boycott the Tokyo Games. In order to spare Japan this embarrassment, he advised to withdraw from hosting the Games. At home, the Japanese organizing committee was also under great pressure. The military showed no interest in the Olympics and ordered that no horses be provided for equestrian contests, as they were needed in the war. Similarly, they requested new constructions for the Olympics to be made of wood rather than metal as the latter was needed for weaponry by the military. Under these circumstances, after two years of preparations, excitement, and criticism, the Japanese Cabinet decided to formally withdraw in July 1938. Tokyo 1940 was abandoned and what would have been the first Olympic Games in Japan became subsequently known as the "Phantom Olympics." Instead, the Japanese celebrated the mythical 2600th birthday of its empire with events all over the country. A central ceremony was staged in Tokyo in November 1940. In June, Tokyo also hosted an international sports event, although much smaller in scale: 700 athletes from Japan, Hawai'i, the Philippines, and Japanese-occupied China competed for five days in regional East Asian championships held in the Meiji Jingu Gaien Stadium.

Japan's Olympic memory: suffering and success

Japanese historians have provided extensive information on the 1940 Games and on the context which led to its abandonment.[3] Museum displays and mass media, however, have treated the "Phantom Olympics" as a stepchild at best while official metropolitan and Olympic institutions in Japan have gone to great lengths to ignore this part of Japan's Olympic history; the official websites of the 2020 Games, of the Metropolitan Government, and of the Japanese Olympic Committee all contain several references to the 1964 Games. In line with the 2013 and 2014 exhibitions in the Edo-Tokyo Museum, 1964 is celebrated as "an enormous success" that "demonstrated to the world its [Japan's] miraculous restoration." These celebrations continue, such as in Tokyo Governor Koike's opening of a 2019 Olympic exhibit at the museum (see Figure 18.2). In its only reference to 1940, the Japanese Olympic Committee explains, "the Japanese government decided to forfeit the Tokyo Olympics after becoming

Figure 18.2 Governor Koike (with former professional tennis player Matsuoka
         Shuzo) at opening of Sport and Olympic exhibit, Edo-Tokyo Museum,
         2019.
Source: © Torsten Weber.

embroiled in the Sino-Japanese War."[4] This choice of wording which suggests that Japan was a victim of the war, rather than its perpetrator, is not uncommon. The Olympics exhibition at the Tokyo Metropolitan Library uses similar euphemistic language to conceal the active role of Japan's military and government in the war against China. Its historical timeline, which accompanies the display of books, an Olympic shirt, and an original torch from the 1964 relay, explains that Japan returned the hosting right "under the influence of the Sino-Japanese War." Questioned about the lack of contextualization of the forfeited Games, a curator of the exhibition replied that "there was no space to include more on 1940."

The story takes a turn when looking at how the aforementioned Showakan museum deals with the Olympics. The Showakan is sponsored by the Japanese Ministry of Health, Labor, and Welfare and focuses on "the hardships of the Japanese people in daily life" during the war and in the immediate postwar years. It is frequently criticized for its lack of international and political context and for its emphasis on Japanese victimhood. As one could expect, its 2019 Olympic exhibition focuses on 1964: the infrastructural preparations, the impact on the life of Tokyoites, and the sports event. However, roughly a quarter of the exhibits does deal with 1940 and displays official documents, promotional pamphlets and souvenirs. The latter include a child's kimono with Olympic motifs, teacups

(*Orinpikku 2600 Tokyo*), and a collector's badge to celebrate Tokyo's winning bid. Most of the items were produced in 1936, immediately after Tokyo had been chosen to host the next Games. Text panels explain how in the context of the war in China, the domestic mood turned against the Olympics. The military's refusal to let their horses participate is mentioned, as is the fate of 35 Japanese Olympic athletes who lost their lives as soldiers in the war.

Victimhood and pride: when wartime and postwar merge

The Showakan exhibition reveals something quite remarkable about the links between Japan's wartime and postwar and how both periods merge in public commemoration; the revisionist stance taken by this museum on Japan's wartime past enables it to openly address the war, albeit in a way that ignores Japanese aggression and war guilt: the same Japanese that suffered during the war successfully rebuilt the country a decade later. In fact, there are many continuities and similarities in symbolism, personnel, and practicalities between the 1940 and 1964 Olympics. As historian Sandra Collins writes, "the Tokyo campaign for the Olympics [in the 1950s] differed only slightly from its 1930s predecessor in the quality of the political purposes of defining Japanese culture within the context of the Olympic Games."[5] Both in 1940 and 1964, the Olympics were meant as displays of Japan's modernity and advancement on equal footing with the West and its superiority in Asia. After all, Tokyo in 1964 was the first city in Asia to host the Games – as it would have been in 1940. Tokyo's governor Azuma Ryotaro (1893–1983), who enthusiastically supported Tokyo's 1964 bid, had been a member of the City Assembly that had promoted Tokyo's 1940 bid. The football, wrestling, hockey, and volleyball competitions in 1964 were held in Komazawa Olympic Park, which had initially been planned for the 1940 Games. The torch relay in 1964 was based on the plan of the 1940 route. And as he probably would have done in 1940, Emperor Hirohito opened the 1964 Games. Other symbols remained the same as well: *Kimigayo* and *Hinomaru* as Japan's de facto national anthem and national flag. To the Japanese, they may have symbolized pride in Japan's success of postwar recovery after the destruction and defeat in World War II. But to their Asian neighbors who had been the victims of Japan's imperialism, these symbols were and are still today reminders of oppression, aggression, and the lack of repentance. This absence of a clear-cut break between Japan's wartime past and postwar Japan is rather symptomatic of the country's approach to its difficult past, not only in practice but also in memory.

Notes

1 For Japan's dealing with its wartime past, see Hashimoto, Akiko. 2015. *The long defeat. Cultural trauma, memory, and identity in Japan.* Oxford: Oxford University Press; Kingston, Jeff. 2013. *Contemporary Japan. History, politics, and social change since the 1980s.* Chichester: Wiley-Blackwell.
2 The forfeited 1940 Olympics are usually referred to as *maboroshi no Orinpikku* in Japanese, which translates into English as "Phantom Olympics."
3 See virtual exhibition on the Olympics by the Japan Center for Asian Historical Records (www.jacar.go.jp/seikatsu-bunka/p06.html) and Hamada, Sachie. 2018. *Tokyo Orinpikku no tanjō. 1940nen kara 2020nen e* [Birth of the Tokyo Olympics]. Tokyo: Yoshikawa Kobunkan.
4 www.joc.or.jp/english/historyjapan/kano_jigoro04.html.
5 Collins, Sandra. 2007. *The 1940 Tokyo Games: The missing Olympics.* Abingdon: Routledge: 181.

19 Upgrading Tokyo's linguistic infrastructure for the 2020 Games

Peter Backhaus

Multilingualism is not an Olympic discipline, but if it were, Tokyo would certainly deserve a medal. As part of the officially proclaimed concept of *omotenashi* (hospitality), administrative agents in and around the metropolitan region have taken great pains to linguistically prepare the city for the 2020 Summer Games. And they are well-advised to do so, since official estimates calculate a total number of up to 40 million inbound tourists to Japan in 2020.

Monolingual 1964

Back in 1964, the situation could not have been more different. When Tokyo first hosted the Summer Olympic Games, the number of foreign visitors was so small that the organizers apparently did not give much thought to their linguistic needs. In total, the event drew no more than 50,000 people from abroad, 9,000 participating athletes already included. Even though the Games did motivate various larger infrastructure projects, among them the completion of the Tokaido Shinkansen bullet train, it seems that language issues were not on the agenda.

The linguistic infrastructure before, during, and after Tokyo 1964 was by and large monolingual. The few concessions to non-Japanese visitors at the time included some bilingual signage around the sports venues and a set of 20 pictograms, then named *shiruetto* ("silhouettes"), to indicate the various sports that were represented at the Olympics.[1] Even well into the early 1980s most public signs were monolingual. Here is one episode that captures the overall situation: In October 1982, an American tourist was knocked down by a car while crossing a street in Tokyo's Minato Ward. The "no crossing" sign at this particularly dangerous spot was in Japanese only. In response to the accident, the local Azabu police station decided to set up Japanese-English warning signs at this and another 15 spots across the ward. The attention this comparatively small event received – several national newspapers dedicated whole articles to the initiative – testifies to the news value of bilingual signage at the beginning of the 1980s.

Between summit and soccer

An important momentum for the promotion of multilingual signs was the Tokyo G8 Summit in May 1986. In July 1985 the Ministry of Construction had announced plans for a nationwide replacement of Japanese-only road signs within ten years. A model project for the metropolitan region was initiated in November 1985. The scope of the project was to set up 770 Japanese–English signs on expressways in the larger metropolitan region and on surface roads in the center of the city. While still small-scale in scope, this can be considered one of the earliest administrative programs for turning Tokyo into a more "readable" place to foreign visitors.

In 1989 the Tokyo Metropolitan Government (TMG) started summarizing the internationalization policies of its agencies and the lower administrative levels. Their annual reports detail the instalment of bilingual road signs, street block signs and area maps, bus and subway signs, evacuation area signage, explanation plates at pedestrian lights, signs informing about garbage disposal procedures, guidance signs inside administrative buildings, and many more. A review of these documents suggests that by the end of the 1990s bilingual signs in the streets of Tokyo were becoming a sight much less extraordinary than they had been only a decade earlier.[2] Taken together, the metropolitan area spearheaded many developments that were later followed by other administrative regions across Japan. A certain time-lag between urban and rural environments persists to the present day.

Around the turn of the century, we witness another linguistic novelty: the occurrence of Japanese-English signs with additional translations in Chinese and Korean, most notably signs on evacuation and emergency procedures in all four languages. One likely motivation for the new visibility of Chinese and Korean was another major sports event, the 2002 Soccer World Cup, which was jointly hosted by Japan and South Korea. The new focus on the languages of Japan's neighboring countries also reflects an increased awareness – and acknowledgment – of Japan's two oldest and largest linguistic minorities: speakers of Chinese and Korean.

Getting ready for 2020

In 2014, one year after Tokyo had won the bid for the 2020 Games, the "Bureau of Olympic and Paralympic Games Tokyo 2020 Preparation" (official English name) was established as a new agency within the

Metropolitan Government. Among other things, the Bureau has been in charge of further promoting Tokyo's linguistic infrastructure and making the city more easily accessible to the millions of foreign visitors expected for the event. The various activities are summarized at www.2020games. metro.tokyo.jp/multilingual/examples/index.html.

One recent initiative by the Bureau is the Eat Tokyo Campaign. At a specifically designed website, restaurants and related businesses registered in Tokyo can create their own tailor-made menus in up to 13 languages. Based on these data, the site also functions as a multilingual search engine for foreign tourists to find a restaurant of their choice (www.menu-tokyo. jp/). Eat Tokyo also offers a set of pictograms related to eating and drinking, and so-called "communication sheets" with simple phrases that can be used in interaction with foreign customers. This outreach to the private sector, where it is much harder to coordinate language issues, constitutes a pioneering step towards spreading multilingualism beyond the scope of official agencies.

Also noteworthy in this respect is the Bureau's promotion of VoiceTra, a smartphone application that translates verbal communication between

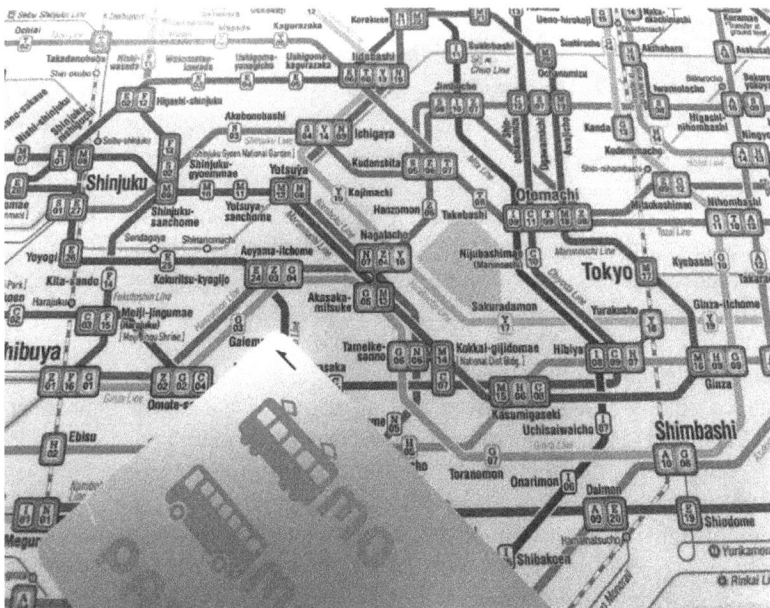

Figure 19.1 Train stations depicted on the English-language subway map.
Source: © Barbara Holthus.

Japanese and non-Japanese speakers. Downloadable free of charge, it presently supports a total number of 17 languages (http://voicetra.nict.go.jp/en/index.html). Technical innovations like VoiceTra may one day present a feasible solution to language problems where they hurt most: in one-on-one situations between individuals.

An entirely different approach to multilingualism is information provision that does not rely on language at all. An example already mentioned is pictograms, such as those developed by the EcoMo Foundation, the additional items from the Eat Tokyo campaign, and, most recently, a set of standardized symbols explaining Japan's sophisticated culture of toilet hygiene (www.sanitary-net.com/global/pictgram/). Another important scheme is the use of colors and numbers to indicate train lines and stations, which can be of great help in finding one's way through the maze of Tokyo's public transport (see Figure 19.1). For instance, where in the past you had to look for Kokuritsu-kyogijo Station on Oedo Line, the National Stadium, you now just head for E25.

The politics of multilingualism

Moving from a monolingual environment to one designed to accommodate larger numbers of speakers with differing linguistic backgrounds cannot be accomplished overnight. Apart from political willingness to do so – no small feat for a society with a strong self-image of ethnic, cultural, and linguistic homogeneity – quite a number of delicate decisions need to be made. Some of them are at least as political as they are linguistic.

An obvious point is the selection of languages. English, Chinese, and Korean can now be identified as the three "other" languages of Tokyo. In road traffic, public transport, and other officially regulated environments, it seems that since the 1990s an English byline has become all but obligatory. In addition, there are now increasingly large numbers of signs offering information in all four languages. The symbolic significance of this new visibility of the languages of Japan's neighbors, on official signs in the heart of the city, can hardly be overrated.

With respect to Chinese, an additional decision had to be made as to which variety of the language should be chosen. The situation is rather complex here, in that mainland China and Singapore use simplified, short-style, characters, whereas Taiwan and Hong Kong still write in traditional, long-style, characters. That the choice was eventually made in favor of the former, at least on most of the official signs, is also a political statement.

Spelling problems

Though much less political in nature, the Romanization of place names is a problem of high complexity. Since two slightly divergent systems exist for putting Japanese into alphabet, it is important to avoid inconsistencies. Official manuals have made a choice here in favor of the Hepburn system, which is taken to be more easily comprehensible to readers with an English-language background. Just compare "Shinjuku" (Hepburn) to "Sinzyuku," which would be the rendition of the toponym in the corresponding Kunrei system. Other specifications on Romanization include the use of hyphens, macrons and capitals, all intended to eliminate irregularities and arrive at a unified set of spelling rules.[3]

Things can get really complex when it comes to the Romanization of place names that combine common and proper nouns. Take toponyms like Arakawa or Yamate-dori. The former is a well-known river that runs through the northern parts of the city, the latter is one of Tokyo's main ring roads. The basic rule is that the proper noun part should be Romanized, whereas the common noun is translated into English. The problem is that in many cases the common noun part has become part of the toponym itself. Just as in our two examples, where *kawa* means "river" and *dōri* "road," respectively. As a compromise, official documents have come to

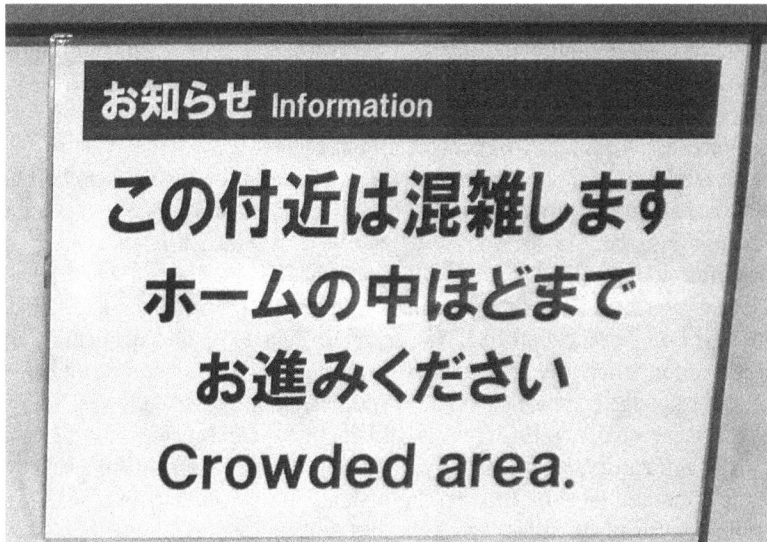

Figure 19.2 Sign giving instructions on how to behave on a crowded platform.
Source: © Peter Backhaus.

recommend Romanization of the full term, added by a translation for the common noun part. For our two examples, this gives us the somewhat redundant but no doubt most easily accessible renditions "Arakawa River" and "Yamate-dori Avenue."

Particularly on signs with more complex or variegated contents, it is frequently the case that translations are provided only in part. An example from public transport is presented in Figure 19.2. The bilingualism here is rather dysfunctional, since the real "information" – that people should move on to the middle of the platform – remains inaccessible without thorough literacy in Japanese. Fortunately, such instances of "make-believe bilingualism" by the eve of Tokyo 2020 have become increasingly rare sights.

Farewell, monolingual Japan?

Signs are one thing; real language competence is another. The gap between the two is particularly striking in domains such as public transport, where written information is now commonly available not only in Japanese and English, but in Chinese and Korean as well. In addition, most train companies in the past couple of years have started using pre-recorded announcements in a bilingual, Japanese–English, format, and here too, Chinese and Korean are catching up. And yet it is still rather exceptional to hear a live announcement in a station or train in a language other than Japanese, except on the Shinkansen. Most of the staff, it seems, do not live up to the increasingly multilingual infrastructure their companies now provide. This is not necessarily a problem, but may well become one in emergency situations such as a major earthquake, where most signs and pre-recorded messages will become all but useless.

In fact, lack of linguistic competence continues to be the weakest link in Tokyo's numerous preparations for the Games. This is also one of the main findings in a large-scale study by the TMG, in which foreign visitors at departure lounges in Tokyo's two airports, Narita and Haneda, were interviewed. Asked about their experiences with issues such as eating and drinking (average satisfaction of 85.3%), accommodation (76.3%), availability of travel information (69.2%), money exchange (63.9%) and a number of others, language competence (43.2%) was unanimously ranked lowest.[4]

As these data suggest, there is still room for improvement in the linguistic infrastructure of Tokyo, particularly when it comes to the thorny issue of communication between individuals. Advancements in translation technology may go some way here, but will unlikely eliminate language problems once and for all. Given these circumstances, Tokyo's efforts in the discipline of multilingualism may not deserve a gold medal yet. But they certainly deserve a place on the podium.

Notes

1 Ministry of Land, Infrastructure and Transport. 2014. www.mlit.go.jp/common/001043229.pdf. Data on pictograms from Mainichi Shimbun. 1964. "20 kyōgi no shiruetto" [20 silhouettes for the sport disciplines]. 14 May: 14.
2 Backhaus, Peter. 2010. "Modernity rewritten: Linguistic landscaping in Tokyo." In Heinrich, Patrick, Christian Galan (eds). *Language life in Japan: Transformations and prospects.* London, New York: Routledge: 154–169.
3 Tokyo Metropolitan Government. 2014. www.2020games.metro.tokyo.jp/multilingual/council/pdf/honpen_doro_taiyaku.pdf.
4 Tokyo Metropolitan Government. 2017. www.sangyo-rodo.metro.tokyo.jp/toukei/tourism/29kekka.pdf.

20 Sexual minorities and the Olympics

Maki Hirayama

The 2020 Olympics and Paralympics are poised to have a significant impact on how Japanese society treats sexual minorities. Since Russia's well-known discrimination against gay people at the 2014 Sochi Winter Olympics provoked worldwide criticism, the Olympics and Paralympics have been opportunities to advocate for sexual minorities.

The Japanese Olympic Committee (JOC) declared "diversity and harmony" the theme of the Tokyo 2020 Games, encouraging various actors to work to reform society. In 2017, the JOC established the "Sourcing Code" for all direct and indirect suppliers, which prohibits discrimination due to gender, sexual orientation, and sexual identity and promotes respect for the rights of sexual minorities. Given the huge number of companies involved, the code's potential impact is significant.

The establishment of "Pride House Tokyo" in September 2018 is another major step for sexual minorities. The Pride House, a center for information and communication for sexual minorities, was first established by a voluntary group at the 2010 Vancouver Winter Olympics. Aided by international networking, similar Houses have been established in subsequent Olympics and Paralympics and other sports mega-events. The baton has now passed to Tokyo, where the House will be jointly managed by support groups before, during, and after the Games, and a permanent LGBT facility is planned as a legacy.

There are also promising legal developments. In October 2018, Tokyo became the first municipality to enact a human rights ordinance that included a sexual-minority discrimination ban. Yet same-sex marriage remains unrecognized. In February 2019, 13 same-sex couples filed a lawsuit against Japan for not recognizing same-sex marriage. One plaintiff, Oe Chizuka, remarked: "It's a good time to launch legal action because Japan is going to be the host country, and in the Olympic Charter discrimination due to sexual orientation is prohibited." Indeed, some members of parliament are moving to establish legislation guaranteeing equal rights for sexual minorities by 2020. Whether this will change after 2020 remains to be seen.

21 The Paralympic Games

Enabling sports and empowering disability

Katharina Heyer

The parallel Games

Many people associate the term *para* in Paralympic to mean paraplegic. Indeed, the history of the Paralympic movement is grounded in the experience of injured World War II veterans with lower limb impairments that used sports as a form of physical rehabilitation. The current and accurate meaning of the term, however, hails from the Greek term meaning parallel, or equal to. This is to highlight the equal status of the Olympic and Paralympic Games: they are hosted by the same city, use the same venues, and are played side by side. Most importantly, they are to be seen as equal in importance, status, and athletic excellence.

The 2020 Paralympic Games, held for 12 days after the Olympic closing ceremony (August 25 through September 6) will come closest to this parallel ideal since the first Paralympics in 1960. Tokyo's Olympic Village is expecting a record number of athletes (4,400) from a record number of countries and regions (160) to compete in a record number of sports (22) and medal events (540). Some of the Games' most popular events are spread throughout the 12 days of competition: on August 26, the day after the Paralympic opening ceremony, competition in seven sports will begin: cycling (track), goalball, swimming, table tennis, wheelchair basketball, wheelchair fencing, and wheelchair rugby. Athletics (track and field), one of the most popular sports, will be held in the Olympic Stadium each day from August 28 to September 5. Wheelchair rugby is usually scheduled to highlight the end of the Paralympics, but this year the popular event is scheduled in the middle of the Games. The Japanese wheelchair rugby team won gold at the Rio Games in 2016, so excitement is expected as they defend their title.

Paralympic classifications and categories: who gets to compete?

Athletes compete in the Paralympics via a complex classification system that is representative of a "Paralympic paradox," which is a tension created between the focus on athletic excellence and physical impairment. Paralympians may see themselves as "athletes first" but must also qualify as impaired enough to compete in the Games. Accordingly, the International Paralympic Committee (IPC), the Paralympic movement's governing body, has developed a classification system designed to ensure "fair and equal competition" among athletes of similar types and degrees of impairment. For example, the popular goalball is played by athletes with visual impairments who wear black eye masks to even out even small differences of impairment among athletes.

To qualify, athletes must meet a variety of criteria: first, they must have an eligible impairment for their sport. Here the IPC has created ten classification categories: impaired muscle power, impaired passive range of motion, limb deficiency, leg length difference, short stature, visual impairment, and three distinct types of muscle impairments that result from neurological conditions such as cerebral palsy or multiple sclerosis. The final category is intellectual impairment, which is most commonly represented in the Special Olympics, but also recognized in the Paralympics. Noticeably absent are deaf athletes: they compete in an entirely separate Olympic event, the Deaflympics, held every four years at a time and location independent of the Olympic and Paralympic Games.[1]

Once athletes demonstrate that they have an eligible impairment, they must also meet the minimum disability criteria of their sport. The minimum disability criteria ensure that the impairment causes an activity limitation in that particular sport or discipline. In addition, each Paralympic sport defines for which impairment groups they provide sporting opportunities. While some sports include athletes of all impairment types, such as swimming, others are specific to one impairment type.

The third and final step assigns athletes into a sport class, which groups athletes with similar activity limitations together for competition. Sport classes differ by sport, and they can also include athletes with different impairments if these impairments cause similar activity limitations. Some sports, like powerlifting, have only one sport class, while others, like para athletics, end up with 52 classes across different disciplines that include athletes from all of the ten recognized impairments.

The ultimate goal behind this elaborate sorting and qualification process is to minimize the impact of impairment classifications on athletic performance and competition. The assumption is that if athletes are sufficiently similar in terms of the type and level of their impairment, the competition will be able to measure actual athletic ability, training, and talent, rather than giving advantages to specific impairments. As a result, the IPC is walking a fine line between creating categories that are narrow enough so that individual impairments are not the deciding factor in outcome, while also keeping categories broad enough to create competitions with enough contestants that meet Olympic goals of sustainable competition. This tension has increased as the IPC works towards strengthening the Paralympic brand by attracting corporate sponsors, developing merchandising, and selling TV coverage. Broadcasters are increasingly pushing for a streamlining of competition categories to increase ticket sales and improve spectator experiences, which may result in future reforms to this elaborate classification system.

"We're the Superhumans": Paralympic athletes as inspirational and bionic heroes

The 2016 Games in Rio marked a highlight for the Paralympic movement by producing an award-winning media campaign ("We're the Superhumans") that promoted images of Paralympic athletes as inspirational and superhuman heroes. In many cases Paralympians transcend human potential with their assistive devices that can cross the line from therapeutic to performance-enhancing. Nobody is better known for this phenomenon than South African sprinter Oscar Pistorius whose "cheetah" prosthetic legs generated controversy when he qualified to compete as the first double amputee runner for both the Olympic and Paralympic Games in 2012. It is this distinction that maintains the boundary between the Olympic and Paralympic movements. Paralympic athletes are expected to display extraordinary athletic skills, but not outperform their nondisabled peers with bionic devices.

The policing of boundaries between impairment and non-impairment is a central role of the IPC, as it underscores the very purpose of having a separate, or parallel set of Games. And yet, the distinction between "disabled" and "nondisabled" bodies is becoming increasingly blurred and complicated. Don't we all, at some point in our lives, rely on technologies or medical interventions that will assist our hearing, vision, heart function, or emotional well-being? The insistence on these separate categories is reminiscent of similar boundary-making by the International Athletics Federation making distinctions between male and female athletes. South African Olympian Caster Semenya was recently ordered to take testosterone-suppressing hormones if she wanted to continue competing in the women's track event. Her naturally high levels of testosterone were ruled an unfair advantage over other female athletes – much like a set of bionic legs would always outperform "human" ones. The international outrage following the ruling should give pause to reflect on the fluid categories we all inhabit. Will the Paralympians ever transcend their impairment categories?

Paralympic legacies: "to inspire and excite the world"

Olympic legacies are often considered by numbers of world records, ticket sales, or the volume of media coverage. When it comes to Paralympic legacies, however, organizers focus on social change: the ways that the Games can challenge stereotypes and transform attitudes, raise awareness about para sports, break down social barriers, and generally promote the inclusion of people with disabilities in all aspects of social life. After all, the Paralympic movement's central mission does not only focus on sporting excellence, but also on para athletes' ability to "inspire and excite the world" towards a "more equitable society."

There is some evidence that Paralympic Games may have a positive effect on disability awareness in the host country. In Tokyo, several hands-on events have been held in the lead-up to the Games to raise excitement about Paralympic sports (see Figure 21.1). Surveys of previous Paralympic Games in London (2012) and Beijing (2008) have revealed a positive change in attitudes about disability.[2] Most of the studies done on Paralympic legacies find that this effect is temporary and limited to more highly educated and urban viewers, however. The happy exception are children, who take to the Paralympic movement with gusto and will rank Paralympians higher than Olympic athletes in their ability to "inspire and excite." It is more difficult to measure long-lasting effects of this disability awareness, especially regarding improved infrastructure, job opportunities, and equal education rights.

This is especially crucial in a host country with a long and complex history of disability stigma and discrimination. Japanese culture has traditionally viewed certain disabilities as a form impurity (*kegare*) that resulted in the mandatory segregation into residential facilities and, until the modern era, kept people with certain disabilities out of the public sphere. Families were expected to hide their disabled family members like a shameful secret. The 1970s saw a growing disability rights movement affirming disability pride and the right to live independent lives in the community with the help of personal attendants. Japanese disability activists joined a global movement for disability education rights, equal employment opportunities, and an accessible public sphere. They point to the promise of full inclusion and the fact that international comparisons have Japan lagging behind in integration efforts.

Figure 21.1 Hands-on experience of wheelchair basketball at "2 Years to Go" promotional event, 2018.

Source: © Barbara Holthus.

When the 1964 Paralympic Games were held in Tokyo, Japan's disability community flourished in the "hope, courage, and self-confidence" of the Games.[3] The 1964 Games brought international awareness to all Japanese athletes, but especially to Paralympians who were surprised and inspired by fellow athletes from around the world who held jobs, went shopping, liked to have a drink, and lived in their communities. In the words of Watanabe Fujio and Igari Yasunori, the first Japanese medalists in doubles table tennis, "they were like everyone else."

If the possibility of equal status was the legacy of the 1964 Games, the 2020 Paralympic legacy might lead to true inclusion. To that end, the Japanese government has spelled out concrete goals for its 2020 Paralympic legacy. One has to do with using the healthcare support systems developed for Paralympians as models for improving the country's public health system. Another has to do with accessible transportation in anticipation of having an estimated 1,800 wheelchair athletes move around the city. In preparation for the Paralympics, Japan also revised its "barrier-free" public accommodations access plan to increase the number of wheelchair accessible hotels and inns. When it comes to improving access to event sites, Tokyo has launched a Robot Project to assist wheelchair users with navigating the event sites, demonstrating its future in human service robots.[4]

Despite these comprehensive accessibility plans, many disability organizations are increasingly skeptical of the government's promise of the 2020 legacy. Restaurants, especially Japanese-style pubs (*izakaya*) and cafes, as well as shops and hotels are notoriously inaccessible, and guide dogs are routinely barred from public places. Japanese law already mandates the accessibility of public spaces, and while the world attention on Tokyo might prompt some initial attention to these promises, there is a fear of the "2021 problem;" of life after the Olympics. A large part of the 2020 Paralympic legacy might be the strength with which the Japanese disability movement can hold the government to its promise of a "barrier-free" society.

What will Tokyo 2020 tell us about disability in Japan?

The Paralympics reveal a dual picture of disability in Japan. On the one hand, Japanese technology regarding access and assistive devices is highly advanced and increasingly used not only by Japanese people with disabilities but also by the growing aging population. In addition, Japan was one of the first countries to sign the 2006 United Nations Convention on the Rights of Persons with Disabilities, a comprehensive human rights treaty that prohibits all forms of discrimination, mandates disability accommodation as a form of equality, and spells out the path for full inclusion into all aspects of society.[5] It took more than six years for the Japanese government to ratify the treaty in 2014: comprehensive legal reforms had to be passed to lay the groundwork for ratification. In that process, Japan passed antidiscrimination laws, provided for disability protection in education and employment, strengthened its commitment to Universal Design, and removed barriers from voting rights.

These formal guarantees, along with the increased disability awareness raised by the Paralympic Games provide important opportunities for Japanese disability activists who continue to battle powerful social and cultural barriers towards inclusion. Disability is still treated with either ignorance, indifference, or even aversion by many Japanese who have little everyday contact with disabled people. The 2016 murder of 19 people with developmental disabilities living in a Kanagawa care home highlights the continuing stigma associated with disability. It was Japan's second deadliest mass killing since World War II, but none of the names of the victims were released to protect families from having to reveal the stigma of having a relative with a cognitive disability. Japan's experience with disability stigma is not unique: it is a shared history that only slowly emerges from decades of institutionalization and segregation. Like the first generation of Paralympians who were inspired by fellow athletes claiming their rightful place in the world, so will today's athletes carry the hopes – if not to say the torch – of social change towards disability in Japan.

Notes

1 The Summer Deaflympics were last hosted by Turkey in 2017; the 2021 Games will be held in either Los Angeles or Dubai.
2 Pappous, Athanasios Sakis, Christopher Brown. 2018. "Paralympic legacies: A critical perspective." In Brittain, Ian, Aaron Beacom (eds). *The Palgrave handbook of Paralympic studies*. London: Palgrave Macmillan: 647–664.
3 Frost, Dennis. 2012. "Tokyo's other games: The origins and impact of the 1964 Paralympics." *The International Journal of the History of Sport* 29(4): 619–637.
4 www.paralympic.org/news/tokyo-2020-games-robots-unveiled.
5 Heyer, Katharina. 2015. *Rights enabled: The disability revolution, from the US, to Germany and Japan, to the United Nations*. Ann Arbor: University of Michigan Press.

22 Sex in the city

Maki Hirayama

Sports mega-events have tended to be opportunities for an increase in sex work. Tokyo 2020 will also see a significant number of tourists looking for sexual services. Yet in contrast to what had been on offer in previous Olympic host cities, they may be in for a surprise. Japan's Anti-Prostitution Act of 1957 bans prostitution, defined as "vaginal intercourse," thus sexual services generally offer a range of options that include "anything but," such as fantasy-cosplay or erotic massages. And even in Tokyo's most famous red-light district Kabukicho, tourists will not find many flashy advertisements for erotic services since a clean-up campaign has pushed them into the back-streets. Instead, new services aided by the development of the Internet such as *deriheru* ("delivery health"), in which women are delivered to customers' locations, have increased dramatically since the 2000s. This system is criticized for women being more likely to be put in danger than in salons, where staff can guard them, and it creates difficulties in surveilling and controlling the activities of foreign sex workers and traffickers. However, it is expected that most Japanese sexual commerce agencies will not seek earnings from foreign tourists even during Tokyo 2020, because these tourists would likely expect intercourse and thus cause "problems."

Ironically, the expansion of Internet-based sexual services has negatively impacted Japan's "love hotel" business, and here foreign tourists may actually provide the key to their revival. Love hotels offer rooms to be rented usually on an hourly basis for couples to have sex and have recently attracted interest from tourists. The unusual appearance of love hotels ranges from outdoor design like castles to often very kitschy interior designs of windowless rooms with extravagant themes. Many of the love hotels were built in the 1970s, which suggests a liberated playfulness in Japanese sexuality during this period. However, in recent times love hotels have suffered from declining patronage from their conventional clientele due to changes in the sex industry like *deriheru*, which have caused them to become hotspots for sex workers and less attractive to average couples. In response, some hotels have actively welcomed foreign tourists, even introducing reservation systems connected to major online sites such as booking.com and employing English-speaking staff. During the 2020 Games, the capacity of general hotels will not be sufficient, so love hotels are expected fill the niche, possibly creating another evolution in this business.

23 Games of romance?

Tokyo in search of love and Unity in Diversity

Nora Kottmann

"Who will you watch the Tokyo Olympics and Paralympics with?"

This is the title of a short promotional video released by the Tokyo Metropolitan Government (TMG) in February 2018. The story unfolds as follows: A young couple passes through a magical gate to the past where they see their grandparents as a young couple in 1964 – the last time Tokyo hosted the Olympic Games. The young "grandfather" invites the young "grandmother" to watch the Games together and puts a ring on her left ring finger. While black and white impressions of the 1964 Olympics stream in the background, a voice-over narrator explains that the grandparents used the 1964 Olympics as a chance to get married and start a family. The video then returns to the present where we see the young couple enjoying the wedding party of a male friend. Next, we see the woman visiting a female friend – a now clearly married woman with a toddler – "who had always said it's more relaxing to be alone, but who now looks very happy." The grandparents then appear again, now as senior citizens, experiencing the "excitement of the Olympics for a second time." The final scene starts with a close-up of the young couple. They turn their heads toward each other, asking "Shouldn't we as well …?" The video, which is available online, is the government's attempt to "support individuals who want to get married and make their dreams come true by the start of the Tokyo Olympics in 2020. Moreover, it aims to enhance the institution of marriage in society as whole."[1]

"Rushing to get married by the 2020 Olympics" is a common refrain that is found in popular manga- and TV-series as well as in advertisements for matchmaking companies. Connecting the Olympics with a range of issues – as well as products – is not as surprising as it might seem at first glance. In fact, the 2020 Olympics are already ever-present in Tokyo, from the official Olympic merchandise to the ever-increasing

"Tokyo 2020" taxis, as well as yoghurt or candy bars emblazoned with the Olympic rings. Yet, the TMG video sheds light on a critical issue: Japan, as with many other post-industrial societies, is facing serious demographic change. The plummeting of the fertility rate far below replacement level has been caused by a decline in the marriage rate – children born out of wedlock are rare at around 2% – which has become a topic of great concern among politicians, journalists, and the general public. The official handling of the topic in the run-up to the Tokyo Olympics offers a useful perspective on the concept of Unity in Diversity, a cornerstone of the 2020 Tokyo Games' vision, and how it connects with discussions of social change in Japan.

Tokyo's Couple Story: (not) getting married

Getting married and starting a family with a highly gendered division of labor was the norm in postwar Japan and was reflected in the extremely high marriage rates. However, in the last 30 years marriage behavior has changed significantly: More and more adults are getting married later or not at all. At present, the average age at first marriage is 29.4 years for women and 31.1 years for men, and the permanent single rate is 14.1% for women and 23.4% for men, with even higher rates for Tokyo. According to forecasts, this trend will continue, and Japanese scientists are anticipating the emergence of a "Hyper-Solo Society."[2] As early as the 1990s, the Japanese government adopted numerous countermeasures with the buzzwords "reconciliation of work and family," "gender equality," and later on "work-life balance." These policies were intended to discourage women from postponing or refusing marriage.

Around the turn of the millennium, however, research showed that despite the fact that almost 90% of adults had the desire to marry, they were not able to do so for various reasons, the most common being the inability to find an appropriate partner. Within this context, the commercial matchmaking industry started to boom. Concurrently, Japanese local communities and municipalities began officially promoting various events under the label of "marriage hunting." These events are the predecessors to the promotional video discussed earlier, as well as two other initiatives that TMG launched in March 2017 (Tokyo Wedding Day) and November 2018. The latter – Tokyo's Couple Story, a carefully-designed and easy-to-access online portal for marriage support – features a range of marriage-related information, upcoming events, as well as the life stories of select married couples with highly diverse lifestyles, most of them with kids. The portal is intended to help those "who wish to get married and realize their individual ideas of 'being together'."

Marriage Hunting Start Day was one event featured on the portal that I was able to attend as a researcher. The event, which was hosted by TMG in cooperation with the Asahi Culture Center, was held in February 2019 and was part of the two-day Tokyo Couple Days, opened by Tokyo governor Koike Yuriko. The official aim of the event – held in an exclusive central Tokyo venue with around 100 attendees – was "to provide a variety of information on marriage hunting."[3] A fashionable female presenter guided the audience of slightly more women than men through the two-hour event. It included a panel discussion – which appeared to be subtly scripted – with two comedians and four professionals from the matchmaking and wedding industries, as well as a lecture. The presenters talked about fears, hopes, failures and successes, dos and don'ts as well as personal and professional experiences while "marriage hunting." While some of the tips were extremely specific – length of fingernails and best sock colors – the overall message of the day seemed to be that "marriage hunting is normal and will help all of us find an appropriate partner." The atmosphere – the trendy, hip event with the sincere, yet almost paternalistic presentation of the subject matter – was startling for me and made me wonder about the attendees' motivations and opinions. I was asked not to conduct interviews or take photos due to privacy concerns, but I overheard the positive chatter of two women nearby, who – assiduously note-taking – gave me the impression that they found the information useful. During the subsequent "event time," the attendees had the chance to be photographed for their online profile, listen to personalized advice from counsellors and stroll around loosely arranged sofas and bookshelves with an exhibition of reading recommendations of "individuals who had success with marriage hunting." In addition, the bookshelves had iPads streaming the "Who will you watch the Olympics with?" video. According to a statement by a TMG official, no further events are currently planned that explicitly link marriage and the Olympics. Nevertheless, the official continued, the upcoming Olympics will lead to an overall positive atmosphere of change and innovation in Tokyo. He expressed his hopes that this atmosphere could support individuals in realizing their dreams of marriage.

Unity in Diversity: the vision

The explicit focus of TMG on heterosexual marriage is quite surprising in the context of the official Games Vision. This vision is built on three core concepts, one of which is Accepting One Another (Unity in Diversity). "Diversity" is here defined as "accepting and respecting differences in race, color, gender, sexual orientation, language, religion, political or other opinion, national or social origin, property, birth, level of ability or other status." The primary reason for choosing "diversity" – a concept that first appeared in Japan in the early 2000s in the realm of business management practices – can be ascribed to the overall restructuring and modernization ethos of the global Olympic Movement at the time Tokyo won its bid in 2013. At that time, Thomas Bach, who had a reputation as reformer, was elected as the Ninth President of the International Olympic Committee (IOC). He strongly pushed the Olympic Agenda 2020 that was agreed on by the IOC in 2014 and which comprises 40 recommendations "to shape the future of the Olympic Movement." Most significantly, Recommendation 11 ("Fostering of Gender Equality") and Recommendation 14 ("Strengthening the 6th Fundamental Principle of Olympism (against any form of discrimination) [with a special focus on sexual orientation]") put a strong emphasis on diversity. The overall importance that is attached to diversity was highlighted in a speech by Bach in 2013: "We embrace [...] diversity. In fact, [...] diversity is part of the magic of the Olympic Games," concluding: "Let us demonstrate the true meaning of Unity in Diversity."

The choice to focus on "diversity" as a core concept turned the term into a favorite buzzword for policy and city planning. The most prominent example here being the four-year plan called "New Tokyo. New Tomorrow. The Action Plan for 2020 (Tokyo First)."[4] The aim is to "create a new Tokyo" and "develop its three faces" – safe, smart, and diverse – by the start of the Olympics in 2020. "Diver-city," an Anglicism combining the two terms "diversity" and "city," is here understood as "a city where everyone can lead vibrant and active lives." Yet, the focus here is undeniably on raising children and caring for the elderly, and therefore points to the same bias as the video discussed above. Of course, "diversity" also plays a key role in the Olympics imagery. The Tokyo 2020 emblems explicitly symbolize Unity in Diversity through "three varieties of rectangular shapes, [...] that represent different countries, cultures and ways of thinking," and the blue and pink mascots are described as embodying the concept of diversity – designers were not allowed to assign any specific gender to them. The color-coding and appearance point nonetheless to clear associations with a heterosexual couple.

Marriage, love and Unity in Diversity: an ongoing search

According to Aoyama Yasushi[5] – member of the 2020 nomination-winning Bid Committee – Tokyo "must demonstrate that it has transformed itself [...] into a mature society of the information age. [...] One, that welcomes people, customs, and beliefs of all kinds and spares no effort to improve the quality of life." The assumption of the broad concept of "diversity" based on the rhetoric of the IOC might be one attempt to do so. However, despite promoting "diversity," a strong focus of policies to enhance marriage can clearly be identified. Initiatives that concretely promote and support other sexual orientations or divergent lifestyles are almost non-existent. Yet, within the framework of hetero-sexual, reproductive partnership, diversity – as well as individuality – is strongly fostered as can be seen in the policies of, for example, the Marriage Hunting Start Day. Diversity of individual needs and desires defined within the framework of partner search, couple formation, lived partnership(s) and childrearing is emphasized. Overall, finding a partner and getting married is promoted in a very modern and somehow "cool" way. With this in mind, we could conclude that TMG, and the match-making industry, do stylize the Olympics at least to a certain extent as the "Games of romance" or the "possibility of romance." In fact, a rep-resentative of a matchmaking company outlined during my fieldwork that the number of people who actively search for a partner and register with a matchmaking agency rises significantly in advance of specific mega-events like the Olympics. This seems to be confirmed by recent data from the Marriage & Life Design Support Company: "Finding a partner" and "getting married" are apparently the most commonly cited goals that respondents want to achieve by the time of the Olympics. In fact, more than half of the respondents named either "romantic partner" and "wife/husband" in response to the question "Who would you like to enjoy the Olympics with?"[6]

However, not only the number of people who cannot get married, but also the number of people who do not want to get married is on the rise. Therefore, in this state of societal change, "new" types of life plans based on various romantic or mutually supportive relationships beyond a "classic" marriage are emerging and, in the context of socioeconomic upheavals, their acceptance is greatly needed. In the future, the various relationship worlds of straight as well as queer people and those who are single, divorced, or living alone will require distinct attention and support. The concept of Unity in Diversity and its subsequent initiatives stimulated by the 2020 Olympics are a positive starting point, but it is as yet little more than a rhetorical device that demands a great deal of further develop-ment. The crucial time period will be post-Olympics, as Tokyo 2020 is certainly a milestone, but still only the beginning. The main question will be if the concept and vision can be kept alive, put in practice and – sometime in the future – truly achieved.

Notes

1 www.metro.tokyo.jp/tosei/hodohappyo/press/2018/02/02/02.html.
2 Arakawa, Kazuhisa. 2017. *Chōsoro shakai. Dokushin taikoku Nihon no shōgeki.* Tokyo: PHP Shinsho.
3 www.futari-story.metro.tokyo.lg.jp/event/report.html.
4 www.metro.tokyo.jp/english/about/plan/index.html.
5 Aoyama, Yasushi. 2017. "Tokyo 2020." In Gold, John, Margaret Gold (eds). *Olympic cities. City agendas, planning, and the World's Games, 1896–2020*, 3rd ed. Abington: Routledge: 425.
6 Marriage & Life Design Support Company. 2018. "Survey 'Who would you like to enjoy the Olympics with?'" https://prtimes.jp/main/html/rd/p/000000 343.000007950.html.

24 The 2020 Olympic mascot characters

Japan wants to make a difference

Jan Lukas Kuhn

Can you remember any former Olympic mascots? How did they look and what were their names? Olympic mascots have been around since the 1972 Games in Munich and while they are an important funding source and a crucial part of Olympic marketing, few leave a lasting impression. However, when Prime Minister Abe dressed up as Super Mario at the 2016 Rio Olympics to whet the appetite for Tokyo 2020, he could be sure that people all around the world would recognize Nintendo's iconic video game character. Japan as self-proclaimed "character superpower" wants to make a difference. Everyday life in Japan is filled with characters: so-called "working characters" that communicate information and "commercial characters" like Hello Kitty.

The Tokyo 2020 Olympic mascot Miraitowa and the Paralympic mascot Someity balance between cool and cute in their appearance (see Figure 24.1). While their Pokémon-like designs equal that of commercial brands, their life-sized costumed variants that attend promotional events resemble *yuru-kyara*, another type of mascot representing prefectures or institutions in Japan. One internationally acclaimed example is the black, round-bellied mascot character Kumamon of Kumamoto Prefecture.

The Olympic mascots' color coding alone, blue for Miraitowa and pink for Someity, is clearly gendered, despite the official statement that they are not. In addition, the official mascot website describes Miraitowa as "very athletic" and having a "strong sense of justice," while Someity is "usually quiet" and said to be influenced by cherry blossoms. Both designs are based on the traditional Ichimatsu "check" pattern which is also part of the Olympic logo. The Olympic mascot's name is derived from *mirai* (future) and *towa* (eternity), while Someity is a portmanteau of the cherry tree *Somei yoshino* and the English words "so mighty."

Both the design and selection process for the mascots were explicitly set up to engage the general population. Both amateurs and professionals were allowed to submit their designs. The final design was decided through a voting process among Japanese elementary school children. They voted for the designs of professional character designer Taniguchi Ryo. Mascot goods went on sale in July 2018, with the total revenue of mascots and other

Olympic goods predicted to be about $140 million. Will these characters remain after the Games end or will they be forgotten like their predecessors? Only time will tell.

Figure 24.1 Olympic mascots Miraitowa and Someity.
Source: © Markus Heckel.

25 Olympic education

How Tokyo 2020 shapes body and mind in Japan

Wolfram Manzenreiter

Welcome volunteers

"Rie, you're late!" The nine-year old girl rushes past her friends waiting at the entrance to their classroom. It is shortly past 8:00. This week it is the turn of the fourth graders at Higurashi Elementary School to participate in the "Salutation Group" (*aisatsu shi-tai*). Since classes start only at 8:30, participation in this extracurricular activity is voluntary – nonetheless the entire class registered. Led by their classroom teacher, the children march out of the school building at 8:14 and line up along the road on the left side of the main entrance (see Figure 25.1). Another class has already taken position on the right side, with the principal and more teachers standing in the back. From now on until the school gate is closed at 8:30, the children and teachers formally greet every child coming to school and passers-by on their way to work, calling "*ohayō gozaimasu*," followed by a deep bow. For the next ten minutes, there's a constant up and down of children's heads, and the downtown neighborhood alley echoes with the children's voices.

"This is part of our Olympic Education Program," explains the principal. "Children learn about the protocol of politeness which essentially is part of a Japanese sense of hospitality (*omotenashi*). In addition, we want to make them aware of being part of the community, and how important greetings and awareness are for social relations. By having the entire school participate, our pupils develop a sense of belonging." "Not just to the school," adds Rie's classroom teacher, "but also to the community. And that everybody can contribute to it, by for example keeping the neighborhood clean. Once a month we call our students to volunteer for the Clean-up Group (*osōji shi-tai*) tidying up the shrubbery and walkways around nearby Nippori Station." Like most of her classmates, Rie is not particularly excited about garbage collecting. "I liked the warm feelings aunties on the road gave me in return for my respectful greeting." Her

Figure 25.1 Advertising the Olympics at the entrance of a Tokyo elementary
school, 2018.

Source: © Barbara Holthus.

friend adds, "It's nice to see how my tree gets prettier with every opening
flower." "Volunteer flowers" (*borantia no hana*) is an adaptation of a
device widely used in primary school education. "For every contribution
they make as volunteers, children receive a flower mark to be attached to a
tree on their poster. By having the tree gradually fill with flowers, they
develop aspirations and a sense of dedication. It enables them to observe
their progress and finally a proof of accomplishment," comments the classroom teacher.

This semi-fictional vignette draws on official reports documenting the
curricular tie-ins between the upcoming Olympics and Japanese school
education in the lead up to Tokyo 2020.[1] Weaving together typical school
values of cleanliness and social responsibility with Olympic themes of volunteerism, achievement orientation, and diversity, as outlined in the Tokyo
2020 Games Foundation Plan, educational programs like these represent
ways that Japanese officials envision linking the 2020 Olympics with the
shaping of its own future citizens.

Olympic education

While for most the Olympic Games are simply the world's largest sport tournament, the IOC has always preferred to highlight its founder's idealist vision of the Games in the service of humankind to promote a peaceful world and the preservation of human dignity. Pierre de Coubertin's ideas about Olympism as a "philosophy of life" were enshrined in the Olympic Charter in the 1930s, stating that "blending sport with culture and education, Olympism seeks to create a way of life based on the joy of effort, the educational value of good example, social responsibility and respect for universal fundamental ethical principles." Making sure that this does not go unnoticed is the responsibility of the Olympic Education Commission. Prior to its installment in 1967, the IOC simply encouraged national Olympic committee members to educate youth about the Olympic spirit. Retired architecture professor Watanabe Kenichi remembers the textbook *The Olympics and school* that was widely used among elementary and junior high schools upon the occasion of the 1964 Tokyo Summer Olympics. However, he falls short of remembering the core principles of Olympism addressed in the textbook, including international goodwill, mutual respect, pride in being Japanese, knowledge about the Olympics, and a proactive attitude towards participation in sports. Fast forward to the present, in which coeval Olympics Minister Sakurada Yoshitaka, whose periodic gaffes enforced his removal in April 2019, confessed in a diet session to neither being aware of the Olympic ideals in detail or having read the Olympic Charter.

Sakurada's ignorance is remarkable given that the IOC nowadays is taking a tougher stance on message control. Ever since corruption, bribery, doping, hyper-commercialization of sports, and the excessive costs explosion of host cities have stained its public face, education and the immaterial values of the Olympics have become a core element of its public relations affairs. Part of the IOC reform Agenda 2020 is the requirement by host candidate cities to outline "educational programmes for the promotion of a healthy lifestyle as well as the Olympic values both in the years leading up to and during the Games." Another outcome is the Olympic Values Education Programme, a resource toolkit packed with ideas, stories, and activities to be used in and outside of classrooms at all levels from elementary to senior high school. Since 2007 it is available in the public domain for free and most of its content has also been translated into Japanese.[2] However, teachers and scholars in Japan found it difficult to use and the teaching of universal principles simply not fitting with national curricula and Japanese customs. Stakeholders such as the Tokyo Metropolitan Government or the Japan Sports Agency at the Ministry of

Education therefore put great effort into developing their own Olympic teaching resources, organizing workshops for teachers, sponsoring the exchange of schools with Olympians and Paralympians, and monitoring the adaptation of Olympic education at the school level.

The official objectives in Japan echo the IOC's current interest as much as the goals from 1964: (1) to promote the significance and history of sport, the Olympics, and the Paralympics; (2) to train volunteers who embody Japan's spirit of "hospitality"; (3) to raise awareness about the notion of an "inclusive society" through sport; (4) to cultivate the public awareness of Japanese culture and to promote intercultural understanding and diversity; and (5) to promote interest and enjoyment of sport. Within Tokyo, and some of its neighboring municipalities that co-host Olympic events, all grades from elementary through high school are expected to devote a minimum of 35 hours per year to realizing these objectives, not just in physical education, but also in political education, history, moral studies, geography, or language classes. In Tokyo alone, about 3,500 schools with 1.5 million students between the ages of 3 to 18 are exposed to Olympic education – until 2020. What comes then is another issue.

Outside the host area, schools are reluctant to subscribe to the promotion of Olympic ideals. Usually, Olympic education is mandatory only at third-year junior high school, where it is briefly mentioned in the national curriculum for physical education. As school education is under the jurisdiction of prefectural educational boards, the central government lacks the power to enforce Olympic education – unless local educational boards are willing to bow down to requests by the Ministry of Education and the Tokyo Organising Committee of the Olympic Games (TOCOG). But TOCOG has found a way to circumnavigate such barriers. Its "Yoi don! School" initiative is targeting all schools and students across Japan. Schools are invited to register directly and participate in the educational program. The meaning of "Yoi Don!" in English is "get set, go!" Get set, go!-schools thus demonstrate their willingness to embrace the Olympic mission, either by having students draw posters, vote for the mascots, adopt teaching material, or imitate the Olympic ceremonial backdrop during their school festivals. As of summer 2019, one out of every three schools across Japan has been recruited. Critical opinions come from teachers mostly, sometimes from parents. Common complaints are about the additional workload with more content crammed into already tightly-packed syllabi.

Outcome of Olympic education programs

Olympic education itself is unlikely to change attitudes towards social participation, voluntary work, or social inclusiveness unless the host government is willing to engage a range of relevant stakeholders and coordinate efforts between different government agencies in a long-term strategy. The same holds true for the IOC's claim concerning increased sport participation as a legacy. Sport participation rates in Japan have been notoriously low in comparison to other advanced industrialized societies. Growth rates over the past two decades were mainly achieved thanks to the increased involvement of the elderly. In fact, no other age cohort has higher participation rates than the 70–79-year-olds. About 70% of them are actively engaged in sports once a week. Adults aged 30–59 are below the national average: about 30% do not participate in any sports activity throughout the year. They feel constrained by tight job schedules and demanding household chores, and probably by lack of opportunities. Past initiatives to promote grassroots sports hence attempted to change behavioral patterns by addressing the scarcity of sports facilities or sports clubs, albeit with limited success. More adults are using their home, nearby parks, or public spaces rather than joining a sports club or visiting a gym. Particularly troubling is the low interest among female teens. Statistics indicate that not doing sports at a young age translates into shunning sports at later stages of life as well.

Stakes are high for the Japanese government that places its hopes on sports and physical activity as a strategy to prevent spending on health and long-term care from spiraling out of control. An active lifestyle not only prolongs the period of vitality and autonomy by eight years on average. It also helps reduce per capita spending. National health expenditures have been climbing in Japan's super-aging society year-by-year, reaching $422 billion, or nearly 8% of gross national income, in 2017. The target of 65% somewhat physically active Japanese by 2022 involves the (re)activation of 20 million people. The Sasakawa Sports Foundation strongly recommends tax incentives and direct investments to achieve such a goal: investments of $400 million are estimated to trigger a reduction of health expenditures by $32 billion.[3]

In recent years, the government demonstrated its capability of shifting priorities and taking a more proactive stance in sports promotion. The establishment of the Japan Sports Agency has been a seminal part of a larger sports policy reform initiated by former Olympics Minister Sakurada during his term as Vice Minister of Education in 2006. Back then, the former rugby player commissioned a report to shape Japan's national sport policy for the 21st century. The "Strategy of a State Founded on Sports" (*supōtsu rikkoku senryaku*) defined sports as a primary policy field of national politics and a soft-power tool to gain status and prestige in accordance with Japan's international importance. It stipulated the responsibility of the government to foster sports by revising the decade-old Basic Sports

Law, to pool political power into a single state agency, and to bid for major sports events. Having promised to expand spending on sports in the case of getting the Games, Japan's sports budget has seen a rise from $235 million in 2012 to $350 million in 2019. However, most of the rise is dedicated to the training of top athletes ($96 million) and the preparation for the Olympics. Expenditure for grassroots sports, including infrastructure measures, lifelong sports and child fitness, is stagnating at a much lower level ($35 million). Olympic education and its ideals of international goodwill, mutual respect and inclusiveness are valuable objectives for sure. But when it comes to the reality of fiscal spending, they ultimately pale in significance in comparison to the real goals of hosting: Japan's National Olympic Committee aspires to see Japan placing third or higher in the gold medal ranking at the 2020 Games.

Notes

1   www.o.p.edu.metro.tokyo.jp/opedu/static/page/open/pdf/teaching-materials/11_article_h29.pdf.
2   "Olympic Values Education" toolkit: www.olympic.org/olympic-values-and-education-program/about-the-toolkit?
3   Sasakawa Sports Foundation. 2015. "Waga kuni no supōtsu yosan no kenshō. Supōtsu yosan to supōtsu kihon keikaku" [Auditing the sports budget in Japan]. Tokyo: SSF.

26　Sex in the Village

Maki Hirayama

At the Rio Olympics, 350,000 condoms were distributed for free. There is an unwritten rule that the athletes can never speak about romance and affairs that occur inside the Olympic Village. Not a few players are said to sexually enjoy Coubertin's ideal of the "garden of youth of the world." For Japanese condom companies, the Olympics is a great opportunity to promote their high-quality "Made in Japan" products to the overseas market. Japan's two top condom companies, Okamoto and Sagami, have been competing to be the supplier to the Olympic Village. They have successfully developed 0.01 mm condoms, the thinnest worldwide. Okamoto products use natural rubber, while Sagami uses polyurethane, which is notable for being "rubber allergy-free" and having no rubber odor.

Why did the development of durable and thin condoms advance this far in Japan? The advanced technology of the manufacturing industry is one reason, but specific tendencies in Japanese contraceptive usage are the main reason. Japan was the last member of the United Nations to approve contraceptive pills in 1999, and even today they represent only a small percentage of contraceptives used. Other more recent methods such as implants, patches, and injections have not been approved, with critics claiming that contraceptive methods that women can use by themselves would "disturb the social order." As a result, condom use accounts for more than 80% of contraception, and the demand for high-quality condoms is very high in Japan.

Nonetheless, over the past 30 years there has been a continuous reduction in the domestic consumption of condoms, from 600–700 million per year in the early 1990s to 200–300 million in the late 2010s. This has been triggered by a range of factors such as the aging of the population, population decline, as well as supposedly overall lower rates of sexual activity in the population. Thus, Japanese condom makers are keen on expanding their market to international consumers.

27 Volunteering Japan-style
"Field cast" for the Tokyo Olympics

Barbara Holthus

Selection process: step 1

On a day in March 2019, a slight drizzle accompanies me on my way to the newly-named Tokyo Sports Square, a large two-storied building in downtown Yurakucho. My appointment that day is to be interviewed for becoming a Tokyo Olympics volunteer, in response to my online application from October 2018. The ground in the middle of the large entryway is painted like a racetrack and I am told to line up on the left side, prominently displaying the large sign "Field cast," whereas the right side is labelled "City cast." 38,000 volunteer applicants had voted in favor of these names that differentiate between those working at the Olympic sites and volunteers guiding foreigners around the city. This morning, only the left side is busy.

With a barcode on my phone, received through the online application site, I am quickly processed and assigned a room in the back of the building. Room names are clearly visible through huge signs hanging above, featuring names of former Olympic cities. Inside "Rome" an MC guides a roughly 200 applicants, all grouped in tables of six, through the first hour. Except for a four-minute PR video, the event is entirely in Japanese. A few foreigners are dispersed throughout the room, who, according to the MC, should be helped by those sitting next to them – a good practice of their English and preparation for what they would be doing anyway at the Olympics. The MC also highlights the concept of *omotenashi*, "Japanese style hospitality," and how much fun volunteering is. After this, we engage in some light activities to demonstrate our skills in communication, flexibility, and decision-making.

I share the table with four women and one man, reflecting the gender imbalance in volunteers who applied, as more than 60% of applicants are women. The man at my table is in his late 30s, works for a global IT company, mostly from his home office allowing him the flexibility needed to take time off from work for the required minimum of ten days – extraordinarily rare for male full-time employees in Japan's labor market. Two of the women are recent high school graduates, who have been living abroad for an extended time. They are ideal candidates for the job: young and with bilingual skills. The ages of the people at my table also reflect the overall applicants, as the majority of volunteer applicants (29%) turned out to be in their 20s and 30s. Also at my table are one woman in her 30s, an English teacher, and a woman in her 60s, a retired apothecary interested in doing medical work as a volunteer. Healthcare is one out of ten fields of action for which one could register upon applying. Volunteers are also needed for distributing uniforms, orientation, staff checks, and security. Most popular, however, are personal support to athletes and the IOC, or working with the media.[1]

Eventually we are split into teams of two to head to the second floor, where we are questioned about our commitment and motivation. After a thorough ID check, then trying on samples of uniforms for the correct size, we are given a token of appreciation in the form of a clear folder with the Tokyo Olympics imprint, a social media ready photo–op and the possibility to leave a friendly message to the Games on a flag, said be used in future promotional events for the Olympics.

The changing face of volunteering

Superlatives and breaking records are a big part of what the Olympics eventually are all about. The same goes in recent years with the number of volunteers aiding in the smooth operation of the world's largest mega-sporting-event: Tokyo 2020 will top London's 70,000 and Rio's 50,000 volunteers with the highest number ever recruited: 110,000 volunteers, including 80,000 Field cast plus 30,000 City cast.

This record-breaking number is surprising for a country where volunteering so far has not been overly popular; well below OECD average in international comparison. The history of volunteering in Japan has been shaped by the heavy hand of the government to facilitate and encourage volunteering and to create an image of volunteering most beneficial to the state, resulting in unfavorable stereotypes about volunteering in the public.

The history of volunteering and respective state policies can be divided into three phases. The first "conceptualization" period from 1945 to 1972 mostly sees governmental efforts for local volunteering, such as neighborhood associations (*chōnaikai*). It is often pointed out that there is no inherent Japanese term for volunteering, instead the English loanword *borantia* is used. This term was first used in Japan in 1964, the year of the first Olympic Games in Japan, but took until the 1980s to become ubiquitous.

The growing knowledge about volunteering went hand-in-hand with a significant image shift from volunteering as "self-sacrifice for others to volunteerism as a means for self-realization and self-fulfillment."[2] In particular, the Hanshin-Awaji Earthquake in Kobe, which occurred on January 16, 1995, inspired a large wave of volunteers to an extent that had not been seen before. Local volunteer groups managed to respond faster to aid the people affected by the earthquake than the government. Since then, subsequent disasters, such as the Tohoku triple disaster of March 11, 2011, and the large earthquake in Kumamoto prefecture in April 2016, also drew large numbers of volunteers.

Besides "disaster volunteering," volunteering to support the state in social welfare work, e.g. elderly care, is the largest field where volunteers are needed. A third category of volunteering is that of crime-prevention volunteering. Despite Japan's remarkably low crime rate in international comparison, a growing media discourse on crimes committed by foreigners aided in mounting fears and anxieties in the population, and thus the number of neighborhood watch groups grew, often born out of the members of neighborhood associations.

Volunteering so far has often not been voluntary in the usual sense of the word. Japan has a large number of neighborhood associations, yet even though in theory participation is on a voluntary basis, in reality, people have an obligation to join and they become members more or less automatically.[3] Research finds that participation in neighborhood associations does not increase the well-being of the participants, whereas participating in "actually voluntary" groups of one's own choosing has a positive effect on well-being. Sports volunteering is such an option. As the fourth main volunteering category, it is still in its comparatively early stages in Japan. As stated above, the term "volunteering" was first used at the 1964 Tokyo Olympics, but the number of volunteers was small. The Winter Olympics, Sapporo 1972 and Nagano 1998, also used volunteers, but on a very different scale. Since 2007, Tokyo holds an international marathon each spring, an event that after ten years draws more than 30,000 runners and more than 10,000 volunteers annually.[4] The foundation of the Japan Sport Volunteer Network and the positive experiences of volunteers in recent years has made recruiting volunteers easier.

Nonetheless, it was doubted if the 2020 Olympics would manage to attract the desired number of applicants, as the Olympics require a very different level of commitment: contrary to the one-day event of the Tokyo marathon, the Olympics guideline is that volunteers have to work for a minimum of ten days. The Olympics are held at the hottest time of the year, making volunteering physically strenuous and challenging. Therefore, campaigns to mobilize volunteers were manifold. One of them was an event I attended in August 2018. Opened under the label "2 Years to Go," many local Olympics sponsors had booths showcasing themselves. At the booth to advertise volunteering one could write a small message supporting volunteering on a sticky note, receiving in return a summer fan with the Olympics logo. The booth was decorated with campaign posters and photos from the 2016 Rio Olympics, showing happy volunteers at work (see Figure 27.1).

In order to mobilize more than a 100,000 people working for free in Tokyo's subtropical midsummer, a change in discourse about what volunteering is and brings to the volunteers themselves was needed. Previously volunteers were motivated by philanthropic motives and aspects of self-development. What is now openly advertised, however, is the element of pleasure: volunteering should be understood as a fun and pleasant leisure activity – an idea very much common elsewhere but for Japan still a new line of argument. The 2020 Olympics wants all social groups, young and old, to participate: from university students to the elderly, from those employed to housewives.

Figure 27.1 Volunteering for the Tokyo Olympics: promotional materials and events, 2018.

Source: © Barbara Holthus.

Eventually, in total, 204,680 people applied for the 80,000 positions as Field casts (the 30,000 City cast positions only drew 36,649 applications). Among them were 81,000 applications filed by non-Japanese, approximately 40%. Time and resources to interview those living abroad proved difficult or impossible in many cases. Results of those chosen to be Olympic volunteers were announced in September 2019, with training sessions beginning soon thereafter.

Shifts in public discourse: between the best period of one's life and the injustices of "black volunteering"

Japanese newspapers have discussed volunteering for the Tokyo Olympics since 2013, and the frequency of reporting started to pick up in 2018. Some articles are nostalgic and refer back to the 1964 Olympic Games, and critical voices are often balanced out with more positive voices. Volunteering is discussed as a possibility to show Japan's spirit of *omotenashi* (hospitality) and as of particular value to introverted Japanese. Also, providing translation and language support as part of volunteering is seen as an opportunity for universities teaching foreign languages.

One of the poster boys of the positivist discourse, highlighting the "once-in-a-lifetime" experience, is Nishikawa Chiharu. In his book and lectures, he emphasizes his positive, valuable, and life-changing experiences as an Olympic volunteer.[5] Yet whereas his and other's reports describe the experience of being a volunteer as positive, the organization, recruitment, payment, and working conditions have become increasingly criticized. These critical voices began to increase in mid-2016. Non-fiction writer Honma Ryu is one of the prominent critics. His evaluation of the unacceptable working conditions for Tokyo 2020 volunteers appeared in numerous magazines as well as in his 2018 book *Black volunteering*.[6] His main points of critique are: (a) the 1,000 yen ($10) per day travel allowance is insufficient for volunteers coming from outside of Tokyo; (b) the working hours of the volunteers (eight hours per day for a minimum of ten days) is equivalent to full-time work – yet without pay; (c) recruiting techniques were emotionally manipulative – and reminded him of Japan's wartime recruiting efforts; (d) the exceptional summer heat and humidity pose a severe health risk to the volunteers and makes for dangerous working conditions.

Outlook

Japan's government hopes to use the Tokyo Olympics to revolutionize the image of volunteering in Japan, to allow for it to also be "fun," to construct it as something positive and to create a "Volunteer legacy." Japan aspires to London's success in creating an active Olympics volunteer alumni network. In such an aging society as Japan, with dwindling funds in the National Pension system, having larger numbers of volunteers can be highly beneficial, particularly, but not exclusively for elder care. "Volunteer legacy" as part of the 2020 Olympics' "soft legacy" tries to make Japan a happier, more social place through "happy volunteers."

However, some journalists in both Japan and abroad have pointed to the stark contrast of the economic interests of the Olympics and their sponsors, versus the "ideal" of the Olympics. Within the ideal of a spirit of friendship and solidarity, having volunteers is "natural" and of utmost necessity to keep the Games running. Yet in a profit-driven world with billion-dollar sponsorships and scandal-ridden Olympic business, to have over 100,000 people work for free with just the "honor" of making the Games a success leaves a bad aftertaste.

Notes

1 https://tokyo2020.org/en/special/volunteer/activity/.
2 Avenell, Simon. 2010. "Facilitating spontaneity: The state and independent volunteering in contemporary Japan." *Social Science Japan Journal* 13(1): 69–93. Page 71.
3 Taniguchi, Hiromi. 2013. "The influence of generalised trust on volunteering in Japan." *Nonprofit and Voluntary Sector Quarterly* 42(1): 127–147.
4 https://mainichi.jp/english/articles/20160229/p2a/00m/0na/014000c.
5 Nishikawa, Chiharu. 2018. *Tokyo orinpikku no borantia ni naritai hito ga yomu hon* [Book for aspiring Tokyo Olympic volunteers]. Tokyo: Ikarosu.
6 Honma, Ryū. 2018. *Burakku borantia* [black volunteering]. Tokyo: Kadokawa.

28 The difference between zero and one

Voices from the Tokyo anti-Olympic movements

Sonja Ganseforth

The scene is captured in innumerable recordings and has come to represent Tokyo – or even Japan – like no other urban view. Every few minutes, the pedestrian lights on the "scramble crossing" in one of Tokyo's busiest shopping districts turn green, dozens of cellphone cameras are raised, and hundreds of people stride across the intersection in front of Shibuya station amidst a cacophony of music and announcements from the surrounding blinking screens and mobile advertisement trucks. On a chilly February evening, a small line of seven cardboards held up above everyone's heads is making its way back and forth through this hyper-urban pandemonium, conveying a straightforward message in Japanese and English language: "2020 Tokyo No! Olympics" (see Figure 28.1).

Behind this tenacious act of protest are a dozen activists from the network No Thank You to 2020 Olympic Disasters Link, short Okotowa-Link, formed in 2017. Despite turning some heads in the crowd, and with two cameramen placed in surrounding buildings to distribute the protest images on social media afterwards, anti-Olympic protest is not particularly visible in Tokyo or in Japanese media.

The Games as a galvanizing moment

Indeed, it is a leaderless group of protest veterans that has joined forces in the movement against the Games. Most of them have higher education and identify as the generation that was politicized on campuses in the 1970s, while being a little too young to have partaken in the student revolts around 1968 themselves. They work at schools, universities, publishing houses, as artists, have retired, or quit their jobs. Some have been involved in the peace movement to protect the "pacifist" Article 9 in the Japanese postwar constitution or in protest against the Japanese emperor system. Others fight for workers' rights, against gentrification and the displacement of homeless people, for the end of nuclear energy production, for the

Figure 28.1 Anti-Olympic demonstration, Shibuya crossing, 2019.
Source: © Barbara Holthus.

rights of sexual minorities, against hyper-capitalist forms of globalization, and even for solidarity with Palestinians.

This multitude of political causes informs the members' engagement, loosely organized in thematic working groups. They hold public lectures and study group events with invited experts, publish reports of the proceedings and occasionally stage public protests such as the street performance in Shibuya. In comparison to these rather intellectual forms of protest, the affiliated group No Olympics 2020 (Hangorin no kai) is more involved in hands-on activism. With a background in defending marginalized peoples' rights, this group assembled in 2013 and has strong connections to the international anti-Olympics movement. Other groups like anti-nuclear movements are also cooperating, with participants joining each other's protest marches.

It is thus a rather small and close-knit intersecting community of social activists, who mostly have known each other's faces for quite some time already from various protest occasions. The Tokyo 2020 Olympics provide a galvanizing moment uniting various social movements: "Even if we knew each other, we did not really organize protest actions together. But when the Olympics were decided upon, we had the strong feeling that people from many different issues needed to come together, because the Tokyo Olympics are bringing to light most of the many problems and contradictions in contemporary Japanese society."

Olympic discontents

Spiraling costs, budget overruns, and the exorbitant use of tax money are probably the most commonly shared criticisms of the 2020 Olympic Games in Japan and around the world. The Olympic image was further tainted by a number of scandals in the run-up to 2020, such as plagiarism of the original Tokyo 2020 logo, the scrapping of the first National Stadium design by Zaha Hadid, and, most gravely, the allegations of bribery in the bidding process.

The anti-Olympic activists raise a range of further objections, some of them concerning violations and restrictions of human rights, such as the exploitation of workers on the construction sites for the new Olympic venues. Another vulnerable group affected by the constructions for Tokyo 2020 are homeless people living in nearby parks as well as residents of public housing demolished to make way for new Olympic structures. No Olympics 2020 focuses on the fight for the rights of homeless and marginalized people. Processes of gentrification and displacement, the privatization of public space and lucrative city redevelopment have been a central concern for anti-Olympic campaigns around the world.

Securitization, increased surveillance, and further restrictions of civil liberties under the pretext of preventing terrorism at the Olympics are other aspects perturbing anti-Olympic activists. For one activist and co-founder of Attac Japan, yet another social movement group, it is clear that "Japanese capitalists are utilizing the 2011 Tohoku disasters and the Olympic Games as a Japanese shock doctrine," meaning a strategy to implement and legitimize unpopular policies such as neoliberal free market policies, privatizations, cuts in social services, or increasing surveillance in times of a state of emergency.[1] The appropriation of the 2011 triple disaster in the Tohoku region in the advertisement of Tokyo's 2020 bid as "Recovery Olympics" is also a point highly criticized by protestors. They argue that the nuclear emergency is far from "under control," as proclaimed by Prime Minister Abe, and the slogan, harking back to golden postwar memories of the 1964 Olympics, is turning cynical as support for most evacuees from municipalities surrounding the wrecked nuclear power plant is discontinued.[2] "Recovery Olympics is actually hindering recovery now, as money, labor, and other resources are now channeled towards the Olympics instead of Fukushima, where it still is needed," an activist explains. One group has made several trips to the Tohoku region to protest ongoing policies and show their solidarity: "The nuclear reactor in Fukushima was producing electricity for Tokyo; therefore, we owe it to the people in Fukushima to oppose Prime Minister Abe's Olympic plans."

With many of the activists having a background in anti-nationalist and peace movements, they also strongly reject the nationalist overtones in the race for medals and the historical roots of sports education in militarist mobilization in the *tennō* (emperor) system. Comparing modern Olympics to gladiator games in ancient Rome, they condemn the inhumanity and consumerism in modern sports events, and criticize the Paralympics as discriminatory for subjecting people with disabilities to the merit principle and performance measures. While the movement consents in the rejection of elite athletics, there is some disagreement on how to assess the meaning of sports for human beings in general. Some believe sports can be a joyful and liberating activity, conducive to human development and a basic right for all humans, which should be fostered through public policies. More radical objectors, however, even speak of fascism when denouncing the notion that sports are inherently good because they supposedly lead to a healthy, long life and reduce medical costs. Reminiscent of Foucauldian critiques of "biopolitics,"[3] they defend "the right to become sick, to live sickly, and to die early."

Domestic isolation and transnational connections

Anti-Olympic protests in Japan are not an entirely new phenomenon. They go back to the bid to host the 1988 Summer Olympics in Nagoya, when extensive local protests might very well have contributed to its failure in favor of Seoul. Before the Nagano Winter Games in 1998, however, critical voices were silenced rather drastically in favor of a "total consensus of the citizens."[4] For Tokyo 2020, OkotowaLink activists feel the public was more critical during the bidding process, but since the positive decision in 2013, most people do not see a point in protesting anymore. Indeed, in a 2017 survey, support rates were as high as 87%. A number of academic publications critically analyze the Tokyo 2020 Games,[5] but the contemporary anti-Olympic movement remains rather small. OkotowaLink's monthly meetings usually have a turnout of around twenty members, while their study groups and lectures attract an average crowd of forty. One activist asserts "I think there are many people who are privately against the Olympics, but it does not become visible as a movement."

In contrast to their low visibility today, social and political movements have a considerable history in Japan. The 1950s saw strong union and strike movements, the 1960s and 1970s were marked by mass mobilizations against the Security Treaty (*anpo*) with the United States, fierce student revolts and university campus occupations around 1968. In the aftermath of the radicalization and excessive violence of Red Army groups in Japan and even international terrorism, social activism was viewed rather suspiciously in the wider public. After an almost 40-year hiatus, however, Japan experienced a new upsurge in movement mobilizations and public protest events with anti-nuclear protests after the triple disaster of 2011. By now, the momentum seems to have died down again, at least their visibility through media coverage. Arguably, the anti-Olympic activists form part of the subaltern structures of a marginalized, yet thriving "invisible civil society" in Japan, persisting from the 1960s, which facilitated the quick organization of recent protest movements.[6]

In contrast to their domestic marginalization, the anti-Olympics campaigners are part of a growing global movement. "With anti-Olympic protests spreading globally, I felt it would be shameful if we did not protest a little more in Japan as well," says one veteran antimonarchist. Especially No Olympics 2020 has for some time now fostered contacts to activist groups around the world and joined the Planetary No Olympics Network. One member even went as far as Rio de Janeiro to support the local movements in 2016. Several OkotowaLink members also joined the protests at the 2018 Pyeongchang Winter Games, and conversely, visitors from other groups are expected in Tokyo in 2020, especially from future host cities Paris and Los Angeles. With international linkages growing, the greying Japanese activists are hoping for more young people to engage during or after the Olympics, particularly as they expect an economic recession after the Games. "The government wants to use the Olympics to make the inherent contradictions in Japanese society invisible, but these contradictions will come out anyways. That's when it will be very important that there are some oppositional voices, even if they are not many." The sentiment seems to be widespread among the movement, giving them a strong sense of purpose: "The difference between zero and one is what counts. That is why we will do our best to oppose and try to get as many people as possible to join in. Well, it is almost zero, like 0.01, but it is not zero."

Notes

1 Klein, Naomi. 2007. *The shock doctrine: The rise of disaster capitalism.* Toronto: A.A. Knopf. See also Boykoff, Jules. 2014. *Celebration capitalism and the Olympic Games.* Abingdon: Routledge.
2 Koide, Hiroaki, Norma Field. 2019. "The Fukushima nuclear disaster and the Tokyo Olympics." *The Asia-Pacific Journal* 17, 5(3). https://apjjf.org/2019/05/Koide-Field.html.

Voices from Tokyo anti-Olympic movements 115

3 Foucault, Michel. 2007. *Security, territory, population: Lectures at the Collège de France, 1977–78*. Basingstoke: Palgrave Macmillan.

4 Tajima, Atsushi. 2004. "Amoral universalism: Mediating and staging global and local in the 1998 Nagano Olympic Winter Games." *Critical Studies in Media Communication* 21(3): 241–260.

5 See for example: Ogasawara, Hiroki, Atsushi Yamamoto. 2019. *Yappari iranai Tōkyō orinpikku* [We do not need the Tokyo Olympics after all]. Iwanami Booklet 993. Tokyo: Iwanami; Nakamura, Yuji. 2018. *2020nen Tōkyō orinpikku no kenkyū: Mega supōtsu ibento no kyo to jitsu* [Research on 2020 Tokyo Olympics]. Tokyo: Seibundō.

6 Steinhoff, Patricia. 2018. "The uneven path of social movements in Japan." In Chiavacci, David, Julia Obinger (eds.). *Social movements and political activism in contemporary Japan: Re-emerging from invisibility.* Abingdon: Routledge: 27–50.

29 Beyond 2020

Post-Olympic pessimism in Japanese cinema

Jan Lukas Kuhn

"Ever since Tokyo has been selected to host the Olympics, Japan floats five centimeters above the ground." This short message opposes Japan's euphoria towards the upcoming 2020 Olympics with mocking irony. It was written by filmmaker Sono Shion, the enfant terrible of contemporary Japanese cinema, and shown in his 2015 "Love & Peace" exhibition.

In his Amazon Prime mini-series *Tokyo Vampire Hotel* (2017), Sono's criticism is blatant. Set in 2021, the Tokyo Olympics did not lead to the hoped-for economic growth and Prime Minister Yamada now promises recovery for Japan, suggesting to distribute microchips to all citizens. In the second episode, in a homeless settlement in Tokyo, a stained signboard appears behind trash bags: "Tokyo 2020: Only 3 days until the opening" (Figure 29.1). Sono puts Olympic euphoria, literally, on the trash pile.

In similar fashion, Kishi Yoshiyuki's boxing drama *Ah, Wilderness* (2017) envisions a hopeless post-Olympic Tokyo. Also taking place in 2021, crime and suicide rates are rapidly increasing. The film starts with a student in debt killing himself with explosives in the middle of Shinjuku. The government reacts with a new policy allowing citizens to pay back student loans by working in healthcare or for the Self-Defense Forces.

Shiraishi Kazuya's *A Gambler's Odyssey 2020* (2019), however, is set directly in 2020. In this reinterpretation of the bestselling novel-series *Mahjong hōrōki* (1969–72), a gambler travels from the ruins of postwar Tokyo 1945 to the year 2020. Encountering stained posters of the Olympics, he is puzzled as the only Olympics he can recall are the cancelled games of 1940. It turns out a new World War devastated Tokyo again and as a result the 2020 Games are cancelled. Implying a possible cancellation of the 2020 Olympic Games was enough to anger government officials. On January 31, 2019, the director and his lead actor Saitoh Takumi were summoned to the House of Representatives for an advance screening, resulting in an unheard-of prohibition of press screenings before the official release.

In stark contrast to the governmental Olympic vision, cinema can present a counter-narrative, addressing the problems of a declining economy, increasing crime and suicide rates, the beginnings of a totalitarian society, and a possible new global war. Cinema brings Japan back to the ground.

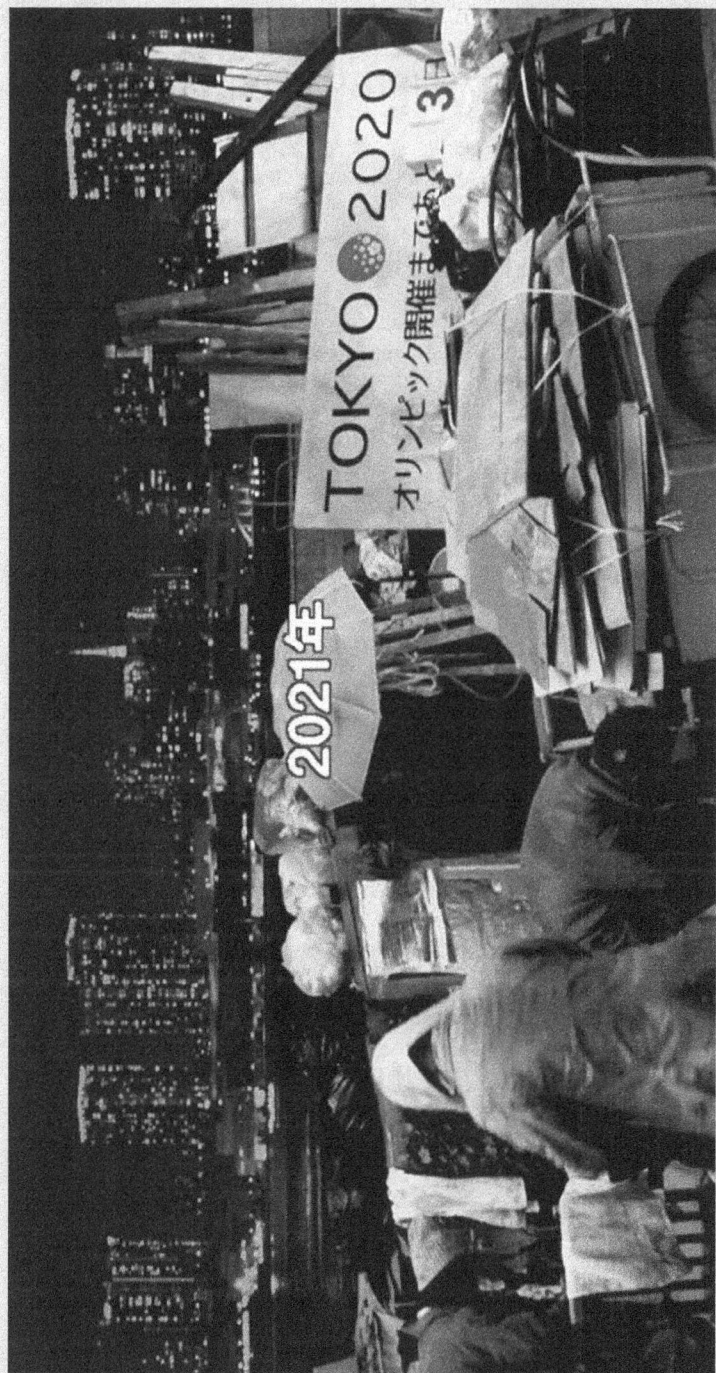

Figure 29.1 Sono Shion: *Tokyo Vampire Hotel*, 2017, ep. 2.
Source: © Amazon Prime Video (screenshot).

30 Tokyo 2020 from the regional sidelines

Isaac Gagné

The Tokyo 2020 Olympics and Paralympics are being touted by government officials and the mass media as an event that will bring the nation together, and as a source of anticipation and inspiration for motivating people across the country. It has also been called the "Recovery Olympics" (*fukkō gorin*), referring to its perceived role in both contributing to and showcasing the recovery of the Tohoku region of northeastern Japan after the March 11, 2011 earthquake, tsunami, and nuclear disaster, known collectively as "3.11."

The 2020 Olympics are certainly a national project – the financial and infrastructural scale of hosting the event has required the mobilization of resources from all sectors and all regions of the country. However, the physical fact that the Olympics will be held in the Greater Tokyo Area means that, with the exception of the relocated marathon (Sapporo), cycling events (Shizuoka Prefecture), and preliminary soccer matches (Hokkaido and Miyagi Prefecture), softball and baseball matches (Fukushima Prefecture), the tangible experience of the Olympics event itself is not national, but localized around Tokyo.

To be sure, the excitement for the Olympics is not limited to Tokyo, and in whatever country the Olympics are held, it always has a national dimension which extends beyond the geographic boundaries of the host city itself. Moreover, Tokyo is massive – the Greater Tokyo Area comprising Tokyo, Chiba, Saitama, and Kanagawa accounts for over 38 million residents, nearly 30% of Japan's population – and thus in demographic terms alone, holding the Olympics in Tokyo makes it a mass national event. And yet, the 2020 Olympics has not been openly welcomed by all corners of the country, especially rural communities still suffering from the 3.11 disaster. So what does the Tokyo 2020 Olympics mean to the other roughly 70% of the Japanese population not living in or near Tokyo?

The view from the regional bleachers

Skepticism regarding the national and metropolitan governments' motives for hosting the Olympics in Tokyo, as well as regarding the purported benefits of the Olympics to areas outside of the metropolitan region, has shadowed the excitement of the official announcement from the beginning. In a 2016 national survey, 31% of respondents from outside of Tokyo worried that the 2020 Olympics would worsen the gap between Tokyo and other regions.[1] In addition, alongside criticisms of the economic effects, there have been vocal critics from the periphery regions, most notably in Tohoku, the northeastern part of Japan that was devastated by 3.11. As of January 2020, over 48,000 people remained displaced due to the nuclear disaster as well as the tsunami that destroyed coastal communities. In the same survey from 2016, 53% of respondents from outside of Tokyo (versus 45% of Tokyo residents) felt that post-3.11 reconstruction has been slowed due to Olympic preparations. And in contrast to the national government's attempts to promote the Olympics as the "Recovery Olympics," 52% of all respondents did *not* feel that the Olympics held value as showcasing Japan's recovery.

The "Recovery Olympics": whose recovery?

The Tokyo 2020 Olympics has been touted as the "Recovery Olympics" since 2012. After the failed 2009 bid for Tokyo 2016, Tokyo's new bid for 2020 began in April 2011, less than a month after the 3.11 disaster. At the time, the governor of Tokyo, Ishihara Shintaro, proclaimed that the Olympics would "cheer up the nation," and the candidate profile submitted to the International Olympic Committee in 2012 characterized Tokyo 2020 as the "Recovery Olympics."

However, for many in the regions affected by 3.11, the wounds are still raw, and healing has been slow. In March 2014, about six months after Tokyo secured the 2020 Olympics, I conducted field research in Natori, Miyagi Prefecture with displaced survivors of the tsunami who were living in temporary housing. Many survivors voiced concern that all of the excitement for the Tokyo Olympics had distracted national attention away from the fact that there were still hundreds of thousands of displaced survivors waiting for their hometowns to be rebuilt. Many also worried that material and human resources needed for reconstruction would be redirected to Tokyo to build Olympic venues. On a research trip to the small town of Zao in Miyagi Prefecture, which was spared from the tsunami but which had many residents who lost family members or had themselves fled from damaged coastal areas, residents voiced similar concerns about the financial strain on the national budget. The plan to have the Olympic torch relay start in Fukushima and pass through the damaged regions also did not draw much excitement among survivors, and some told me that they felt that the region was just being used to gain sympathy for the Tokyo 2020 bid.

In fact, before 3.11 and the Tokyo 2020 Olympics, residents of Tohoku have long had a conflicted relationship with Tokyo and local discourses frame the region as strong-willed and independent but always taken advantage of by the metropole. As the anthropologist William Kelly notes, "resilience, resistance, resolve and resourcefulness have characterized the Northeast from the deep past to the contemporary present."[2] Among the older generations this is particularly so. There is a strong sense that the rural northeast has always been an afterthought to the urban glut of Tokyo, and that the Tohoku people have sacrificed themselves through food production and energy production to supply the bloated metropolis – even as they grudgingly acknowledge that their economic reliance is interdependent, and even as young people themselves increasingly leave Tohoku for Tokyo. Thus, Tokyo 2020 is the most recent spark to reignite these long-standing debates.

The host town project: afterthought or future hope?

The coastal regions in Tohoku that were hardest hit by the 3.11 disaster are the most vocal in their skepticism of hosting the 2020 Olympics in Tokyo, but there are also many other municipalities in the northeastern region where residents feel disconnected from the entire Olympic project happening 300 or more kilometers away. These are precisely the areas that the government hopes to envelope in the Olympic embrace through various "host town" programs (see Figure 30.1).

There have been several strategies for whipping up interest in the Olympics in far-flung corners of the country. The Japanese government has tried to encourage the involvement of communities outside of Tokyo through the "host town" program, whereby a municipality hosts training camps and intercultural exchanges with the Olympic teams from other countries, forging new international opportunities and connections. There is also the "Arigato Host Town for Supporting Reconstruction" program, which aims to encourage exchange between foreign nations that provided support after 3.11 and the local municipalities which benefited from their aid. As of February 2020, 479 host towns have been selected across Japan, welcoming athletes from 163 countries and territories.[3]

These host town schemes offer participating communities a sense of involvement by building direct person-to-person relationships between

Figure 30.1 Palau – Hitachiomiya city host town banner, at Zao townhall, 2019.
Source: © Isaac Gagné.

citizens and Olympians from around the world. Yet the scale of their activities, the level of local interest, and the amount of effort each municipality puts into the schemes vary widely. Most host town applications in Tohoku are initiated by the local mayors, and there is no monetary incentive from the national government for standard host towns. Instead, host towns must redirect their own discretionary funds.

One of the common characteristics among Tohoku host towns is that most reported a general lack of interest in the Olympics and an ambivalent or somewhat negative attitude toward the Olympics itself among residents.

At the same time, the relevant offices in charge of the host town activities in most municipalities were eager to increase awareness about their partner country among local residents. They arranged various speaking events by Olympic athletes, training camps for youth, collaborative school projects connecting local and overseas students, and hosted fairs showcasing goods from the other country.

For their part, host town mayors seemed eager to raise their political profiles and hoped to boost tourism to their regions. However, most of the municipal offices in charge of the actual projects confessed that they saw little possibility of linking their far-flung towns to any post-Olympic tourism boom, especially given the lack of convenient transportation to many of the rural communities in the northeast.

And as for Tokyo 2020 as the "Recovery Olympics," many I spoke with in Natori and Zao in particular remained skeptical and continued to wonder what exactly becoming a host town would do for their daily lives and their communities in the long run. This was echoed in a 2018 poll of municipal leaders in the affected areas, which found that 71.3% felt that the "Recovery Olympics ethos" remained "unclear and unfocused."[4] Indeed, there is a sense among many Tohoku residents that "Recovery Olympics" is an empty slogan that has just co-opted the regions' hardships for the benefit of Tokyo, a sentiment further strengthened by the fact that only 12 out of the 42 municipalities that were seriously affected by the 3.11 disaster were interested in joining the "Arigato Host Town" scheme, with the majority answering that they were "still not at a stage ready to consider such things."

Tokyo 2020: the Olympics as national glue or regional solvent?

So is Tokyo 2020 the glue that will bring the nation together after increasing regional disparities and the catastrophic events of 3.11? Or will it become the corrosive solvent that further separates the shrinking regions from the power-hungry metropole? As the diverse experiences of host towns and "Arigato Host Towns" reveal, the image of Tokyo 2020 among regional residents is not a simple matter of excitement or resentment. The municipalities in Tohoku that are completely disconnected from the Olympic project and have no host town status are likely the most skeptical, or at best the least interested in the Olympics. Likewise, since there are no special funds offered to standard host towns, they must divert their own discretionary funds, which also provokes skepticism among residents, especially in disaster areas.

The positive effects of the host town schemes seem to hinge on the successful engagement of local actors. Rather than being a program linked up with the national project of the Olympics, the host towns in Tohoku seem to be mostly interested in deepening their cross-cultural exchange activities and connections with other countries beyond Olympic sports. In this sense, the host town schemes do not seem to contribute much to making the Olympics a nationally shared event, but rather they seem to be variously adapted to turn the Olympics into local projects for "internationalizing" regional communities by building or strengthening overseas connections, or even enhancing awareness of existing diversity within their communities. Indeed, the strongest impact seems to lie in familiarizing the "foreign" and creating person-to-person ties, especially among schoolchildren and civil society groups.

Ultimately, the view from the sidelines of the Tokyo 2020 Olympics in northeastern Japan may not even be oriented toward Tokyo after all. For many municipalities in Tohoku, becoming a host town does not mean that they are letting themselves be coopted by a metropolitan-centered Olympics project for the benefit of Tokyo, nor that they are hoodwinked by the illusion that Olympic revenues will flow their way in the form of increased tourism. Tohoku residents are fully aware that they are far from center field in the Olympics action. Instead, local actors seem to be looking beyond 2020 to various horizons: mayors to the future of their political careers; sports clubs and companies to the future of international connections; and schools to the future of their students on the global stage. While the 2020 Olympics may not become the "Recovery Olympics" that will restore disaster-stricken regions to their (retrospectively imagined) halcyon pre-3.11 days, for resourceful host towns the Olympics may still be an important opportunity for reorienting local residents' awareness towards the future of their communities in a globalizing world.

Notes

1 Tsurushima, Miho and Saito, Takanobu. 2017. "Expectations and consciousness of the 2020 Tokyo Olympics and Paralympics." NHK Hōsō Bunka Kenkyūjo: Hōsō Kenkyū to Chōsa: November.
2 Kelly, William W. 2012. "Tohoku's futures: Predicting outcomes or imagining possibilities?." *The Asia Pacific Journal* 10, 10(2), March 5. https://apjjf. org/2012/10/10/William-W.-Kelly/3703/article.html.
3 Tokyo 2020 Olympics host town webpage: www.kantei.go.jp/jp/singi/ tokyo2020_suishin_honbu/hosttown_suisin/index_e.html.
4 Kahoku Shinbun. 2018. "7 years since the disaster: A survey of heads of disaster-stricken areas finds 70% do not see the 'recovery ethos.'" March 1.

31 Olympic leverages

The struggle for sustainable food standards

Sonja Ganseforth

With environmental problems attracting global attention since the 1970s, the IOC has increasingly adopted an ecological rhetoric. In line with recent Olympics, Tokyo 2020 organizers are also advertising a sustainability legacy and have formally committed to contribute to the achievement of the UN's Sustainable Development Goals (SDGs) by 2030. Besides financial stability, sustainable energy consumption, and the reusability of new constructions, sustainable food procurement is another important element of the aspirations for a sustainable Olympic legacy. A whole range of interest groups has been struggling to influence these standards before the 2020 Games.

Continuing recent "gastrodiplomacy" endeavors, Tokyo 2020 organizers express ambitions to showcase the excellence of Japanese cuisine (*washoku*) on this occasion in the global limelight.[1] However, there is a considerable gap between the global prominence of Japanese food as soft power and actual food standards. With exports playing only a marginal role in Japanese agriculture, internationally recognized food production and safety standards such as HACCP (Hazard Analysis and Critical Control Points), GLOBALG.A.P. (aka GAP, Good Agricultural Practices), or ISO-based standards remain far from common. The lack in certification is problematic especially for the planned promotion of agricultural and fishery exports.

At the same time, civil society organizations are hoping to make use of the Olympic momentum and have started agenda-setting campaigns. Whether it is whales, ivory, bluefin tuna, or eel, Japan already finds itself under recurring attack from the international community for its handling of natural resources and endangered animal species. Utilizing the increased international attention during the Olympics as a form of foreign pressure (*gaiatsu*), organizations push for more sustainable, environment- and animal-friendly forms of food production in Japan.

Mind the gap – in food production standards

In January 2019, the Tokyo Organising Committee of the Olympic and Paralympic Games (TOCOG) issued its own *Sustainable Sourcing Code*, defining the standards for products and services as well as licensed products.[2] The central document prescribes safety, ecological, and animal welfare standards for the Games, and lists environmental goals but also social and political aspects such as human rights, working conditions, and business practices. Further details are in the individual codes for core products and services: timber, agricultural products, livestock products, fishery products, paper, and palm oil.

The main priorities in the field of agriculture are food safety, environmental protection, workers' protection, and animal welfare in livestock production. With GAP standards promulgated in the *Code*, a TOCOG representative expects the Tokyo 2020 Games will have a long-term effect especially in the proliferation of GAP certifications and fishery ecolabels. However, GAP certification here does not only include the internationally recognized standards but also Japanese variations.

Even fewer producers are certified in livestock than in agriculture. In order to lower entry barriers for producers before the upcoming Tokyo 2020 Games, a "GAP acquisition challenger" status is additionally awarded to producers who have completed a checklist of GAP conditions, without the requirement to actually comply with all listed items. For fishery products, the *Code* accepts weaker Japanese certification schemes alongside internationally renowned labels such as the Marine Stewardship Council (MSC). Further provisions referring to "government-recognized resource management plans" in practice allow the procurement of almost any Japanese product, even from fisheries without effective public resource administration in operation.

Preferential treatment is stipulated for domestic produce in order to reduce long-distance transportation and promote Japanese agriculture, while organic produce as well as production by people with disabilities or "inheriting traditional agricultural systems" is merely recommended. Organic production in Japan is extraordinarily scarce – only around 0.2% of all arable land, compared to 7% in the European Union.[3] Provisions for ecological and animal-friendly food procurement do not go much beyond the status-quo in Japan, and the introduction of Japanese versions of international standards does not constitute a substantial reform.

Struggling to change the agenda

For the preparation of the *Code*, TOCOG assembled a working group with representatives from academia, unions, NPOs, CSR professionals, and the

Tokyo Metropolitan Government. Depending on the topic of discussion, they consulted with other professionals such as researchers, a nutritionist, representatives from MAFF and from agricultural and fishery cooperatives as well as consumers' associations. After many heated discussions over almost three years, and a round of public comments on a first draft, the final edition came out in January 2019. Since the last two Summer Olympics in London and Rio de Janeiro already set the bar comparatively high in terms of sustainable food procurement, the Tokyo *Code* is criticized for lowering the existing standards. Yet a TOCOG representative defends the decision not to uphold the same level: "We cannot easily compare London and Tokyo. This is a point I would like you to understand. We had to look at the current situation in Japan and think about what kind of legacy we want to leave behind with this code."

While internationally recognized standards spread to some degree, there is only a weak "recommendation" for organic agriculture. Organic Village Japan is hoping to promote organic agriculture beyond the 2020 Games by serving local organic produce to athletic teams in regional host towns. Other civil society organizations have been working to reform animal-based food production. The Japanese NPO Animal Rights Center (ARCJ) demanded to include animal welfare protection in the *Code* and to maintain at least the standards of the London Olympics. Practices such as gestation crates, forced molting, and battery cages are now forbidden in the EU, but are still used by most producers in Japan. In 2018, together with The Humane League Japan, ARCJ supported the global campaign of some Olympians demanding 100% cage-free eggs and 100% stall-free pork, calling for a boycott of animal products at the Tokyo 2020 Olympic Games venues otherwise. A few sympathetic parliamentarians are helping to promote the agenda by asking critical questions about animal welfare at the Tokyo Olympics in the Diet. "Many politicians as well as companies are actually thankful to learn about these issues," explains ARCJ's Okada Chihiro, underlining the lack of awareness in the Japanese public and the unfamiliarity of the concept of "animal welfare." She does not consider its appearance in the *Code* a success, as it refers only to very basic private industry management standards. In fact, she considers this tokenistic reference a deception, similar to the introduction of Japanese GAP versions, which falsely seem to suggest the existence of food safety standards on par with international levels.

Similar criticism concerns the recognition of Japanese seafood ecolabels. In an open letter, Greenpeace International condemned the endorsement of weak and inadequate certification schemes: "By doing so, Games organizers will be misleading consumers into believing they are making responsible purchasing decision." Though not reflected in the *Code*, the

Japan Fisheries Association in 2018 submitted a strengthened version of its ecolabel for international benchmarking with the goal of achieving worldwide recognition before the 2020 Games – apparently in response to increasing pressure from environmental groups. This is why Hanaoka Wakao from Tokyo-based consulting firm Seafood Legacy sees a positive impact after all: "When founding Seafood Legacy in 2015, we had Tokyo 2020 as the first big milestone. And I think we are reaching this goal, as many companies are approaching us saying they want to do something in time for the Tokyo Olympics." Different from the rather confrontational stance of many environmental NGOs, Seafood Legacy works with seafood and retailing businesses to make their supply lines more sustainable and to enhance the Japanese sustainable seafood market: "Business needs to change, they also act as a medium to consumers. And policy will also follow business."

NGO pressure, however, is crucial, especially if it is international. Seafood Legacy published its criticism of the *Code* along with similar statements by partners from their international network of sustainability groups and companies in an open letter to the TOCOG. Relations are especially close to organizations in the USA. American foundations like the David and Lucile Packard Foundation aim to "lay the groundwork for a sustainable seafood movement" in Japan through generous grants to organizations including Greenpeace Japan, MSC, WWF, Sailors for the Sea, and Seafood Legacy, in "a coordinated effort around the 2020 Tokyo Olympics."[4]

The ambition to make MSC-certification mandatory in the *Code*, however, was thwarted just like other standards for agriculture and livestock. Pointing out the necessity to source enough food for the Games, the TOCOG representative explains: "For us in the Organizing Committee, it would be great trouble if the procurement standards were too strict and there was not enough material available. We cannot just go for the ideal but have to set standards within an attainable level."

An Olympic legacy?

Animal rights and sustainable seafood advocates are not satisfied with this argument, insisting an "Olympic legacy" in the sense of stricter standards would have been possible, if there were stronger political will and effort. "I think it is a pity that Japan could not use this opportunity to establish higher standards," Hanaoka remarks. For some years already, critics have denounced the ubiquitous rhetoric of "sustainable Olympic legacies" in the absence of any significant environmental or even financial stringency as "greenwashing." Nevertheless, the "rhetorical bandwagon"[5] of Olympic legacies rolls on, from London and Rio to Tokyo.

Coherent with the controversial framing as "Recovery Olympics," TOCOG also highlights the Games as an opportunity to "make the utmost use of foods produced in the disaster-stricken areas," suggesting a return to normalcy after the 2011 nuclear disaster in Fukushima: "Tokyo 2020 will attempt to disseminate accurate information on food safety, put an end to the negative reputation locally produced foodstuffs have endured and communicate the attractiveness of food produced in the affected areas."[6] However, even if voicing concern about radioactive contamination of foodstuff remains somewhat taboo, it has substantially shaken Japanese consumers' trust and highlighted the politically constructed nature of food safety regulations.

Campaigners advocating for stronger environmental and animal rights regulations in Japan pin their hopes on foreign visitors and the expected international media attention. ARCJ has already published a compendium in English entitled *Tokyo animal cruelty* and is likely to continue appealing to foreign audiences before and during the Games. *Gaiatsu*, foreign pressure, is considered an important force in Japanese politics, and Hanaoka is convinced it is also pushing many companies to achieve more aspirational seafood standards in order to avoid foreign media bashing. However, he stresses the importance of applying *gaiatsu* strategically and in coordination with an insider perspective in order to avoid a nationalistic backlash similar to the whaling controversy.

Considering the half-hearted policy concessions and the inertia of official regulations, civil society pressure and business initiatives might indeed be more promising. However, reliance on the private sector comes at a price. Though certainly bringing improvements, market-based certification schemes such as MSC are deeply problematic, none the least due to their inherent business-oriented logic. Similar to retailer-initiated private labels like GLOBALG.A.P., the costly and time-consuming certification process exerts a heavy burden on producers and often excludes small-scale companies. In their agenda setting campaigns, deep-pocketed foundations are promoting specific concepts of sustainability and market-based resource governance, and international hegemonic standards and private labels are exerting considerable power in typically buyer-driven global commodity chains. Ultimately, the contest over food procurement at Tokyo 2020 is played out within the context of global power struggles to define food standards.

Notes

1 The Tokyo Organising Committee of the Olympic and Paralympic Games (TOCOG). 2018. "Tokyo 2020 basic strategy for food & beverage services." 2018.03. https://tokyo2020.org/en/games/food/strategy/data/Basic-Strategy-EN.pdf.

2 TOCOG. 2019. "Tokyo 2020 Olympic and Paralympic games sustainable sourcing code." (3rd edition). https://tokyo2020.org/en/games/sustainability/data/sus-procurement-code3_EN.pdf.

3 Ministry of Agriculture, Forestry and Fisheries (MAFF). 2018. *Heisei 29nendo shokuryō, nōgyō, nōson on dōkō sankō tōkeihyō* [2017 White book on food, agriculture and rural areas, statistical references]. www.maff.go.jp/j/wpaper/w_maff/h29/pdf/sankoutoukei/sankoutoukei.pdf; Eurostat. 2019. "Organic farming statistics." https://ec.europa.eu/eurostat/statistics-explained/index.php/Organic_farming_statistics. Calculated by projecting 9.956ha under organic cultivation to around 4.5 mill. ha arable land in Japan.

4 The David and Lucile Packard Foundation. 2016. "Japan Seafood Market & Fisheries Strategy." May 2016. www.packard.org/wp-content/uploads/2016/11/Japan-Seafood-Market-and-Fisheries-Strategy.pdf.

5 Tomlinson, Alan. 2014. "Olympic legacies: Recurrent rhetoric and harsh realities." *Contemporary Social Science* 9(2): 137–158.

6 TOCOG. 2018: 26.

32 Security for the Tokyo Olympics

Sebastian Polak-Rottmann

Security and the Olympic Games

Mega-events are often associated with potential threats of terrorism and other forms of unpredictable violence. In the case of the Olympic Games, security has a somewhat ambivalent relationship with the core values of the event. As social scientist Don Handelman puts it, surveillance and increasing "militarization and securitization of anything and everything relating to the Games" are a contradiction to the notion of peace championed during the event.[1] In many cases the police work together with military forces and private security companies to cope with the increasingly complex structure of the Games. Some of the Games, however, could not succeed in meeting the high requirements of security: In the case of London, private security companies failed to employ the necessary amount of personnel – something that the Japanese Olympic Committee initially feared as well.

But security entails more than just security guards. It is rather something that "encompasses all kinds of domains of social activity."[2] Thus, security does not stop by just filling security gaps for the event but is rather actively involved in designing the event. Security is also crucial during construction: discussions in the Tokyo government frequently centered around the high amounts spent for the protection of the construction sites.

Of course, a high level of security is nothing exceptional during mega-events. However, how much security is "sufficient?" Security is not something tangible, nor visible, and it is easy to claim that security was insufficient in case something were to happen. In the eyes of the government or the organizers, major incidents during previous events have made surveillance a necessity for future Games. The attack on the Israeli Olympic team during the Munich Olympic Games in 1972 thus effectively shaped the understanding of security as an integral part of the Olympic Games and further catalyzed the enactment of security measures during the Games.[3] At the 1964 Tokyo Games, local administration did not consider security a big issue, but rather wanted to show a positive image of a recovered and orderly Japanese nation.[4] The Winter Olympics in Sapporo in 1972, however, proved to be different regarding security measures. As they took place during the "golden age of social movements" in Japan, attacks from protesters of different political camps inside Japan were feared by the organizers. The Sapporo Games thus helped to legitimize tighter security – mostly to deal with the "enemy within."[5]

To what degree organizers or nations ultimately decide to enact security policies highly depends on potential threats or on past events which showed flaws in their security strategies. Considering the long history of the Games makes it understandable why the security apparatus has become bigger over time. In times of frequently occurring attacks on events and growing concerns about cyber security in the age of digital connectivity exemplified by the Internet of Things (IoT), who is able to provide this huge security apparatus during the 2020 Games?

Securing 2020: cooperation and the pursuit of absolute security

Since 2016, every year at the end of December, the Tokyo Organising Committee of the Olympic and Paralympic Games (TOCOG) presents the budget for the 2020 Games. Security expenses are scheduled to make up around $900 million, 75% of which is covered by the Tokyo Metropolitan Government. Critical responses about too much security are hard to find.

Having the security during the Games in mind, the cabinet of Prime Minister Abe Shinzo announced the "Strategy for Japan as the safest country of the world" in December 2015, aiming to support the belief of the Japanese people in a "strong Japan" during the Games in 2020. In this report, the government lists "new threats" emerging from inside and outside Japan: cybercrime, cyberattacks, international terrorism, and organized crime. This emphasis on different forms of (mostly) organized crimes inside and outside cyberspace led to the establishment of an organization similar to the US NCFTA (National Cyber-Forensics and Training Alliance) and to the strengthening of existing systems. Since January 2015, located in the cabinet secretariat, the National Center of Incident Readiness and Strategy for Cybersecurity (NISC) is responsible for national cyber security. Preparing for the Tokyo Olympics, the NISC has gathered information on the cyber security environment of the previous three Games in London, Rio, and Pyeongchang. The organization refers to attacks by Anonymous in Rio, where both the websites of the government and the organizers had become targets, as well as the attacks on the networking systems at Pyeongchang. The NISC fears that this time around, as the Internet of Things (IoT) is spreading at a fast pace, potential attackers might target these devices in a concerted attack. The NISC thus has prepared numerous scenarios of possible risks and how they might wreak havoc onto the Games. The organization's homepage covers around 70 different case scenarios, including DDoS (distributed denial of service) attacks that may disrupt the internet service of the IOC or related organizations. While the NISC is part of the cabinet secretariat, the Olympic Committee has its own computer security incident response team that mainly engages in risk prevention strategies similar to its national counterpart. Chief Security Officer of the Olympic Committee, Yonemura Toshiro, former chief inspector of the Tokyo Police and advisor to the Abe Cabinet, summarizes the main activities of the planning as "imagination and preparation" (*sōzō to junbi*). He points to the importance of considering all possible risks in order to avoid the unexpected.

In March 2017, the previously established Security Directorial board announced the Main Strategy for Security during the Olympic and Paralympic Games in Tokyo 2020. This strategy introduces measures against threats during the event in more detail. One of the core elements is the establishment of security centers that will operate 24 hours-a-day at the Cabinet Secretariat to ensure a dense informational network during the Games, and to aid the police department in evaluating potential risks. In addition, this strategy emphasizes the close cooperation with private and public actors – something that is mentioned continuously within Japanese security discourse. This is especially interesting when considering the strict regulations for private security companies (PSC) in Japan. As private actors, these companies usually provide services only for the clients of their contract. However, especially during mega-events or natural disasters, the police department frequently asks for cooperation and relies on PSC staff and expertise. In joint statements, officials usually highlight the "important place within Japanese society" or the "responsibility and expectation for their engagement in security" of the private security industry. Even though employees of PSCs are not allowed to carry weapons and do not have any special rights concerning security in Japan, they have become an integral part of Japanese everyday life over the past decades.

During the Games, most of the security tasks on site will be fulfilled by a collaboration between police (21,000) and PSC (14,000), with Self-Defense Forces supporting the personnel. To ensure that there will be sufficient security guards available during the event, Japanese PSC created a joint venture. In addition, Japan's two largest security companies SECOM and ALSOK, who are official JOC partners, as well as several other companies agreed to collaborate. This strategy enables the different companies to effectively spread their staff flexibly to the various Games sites. This avoids small companies having to make their own contracts that would assign them to specific tasks, which would make it harder to react spontaneously to immediate requests. Compared to the previous Games in Tokyo in 1964, this time the venues are located in different areas of the city, which all require high levels of security. A flexible team of security guards is believed to be able to address this challenge smoothly. SECOM and ALSOK are confident that their approach will become a legacy of the 2020 Tokyo Olympic Games. They also hope that the event will further improve the level of the private security industry in Japan, which until now has been struggling with a bad reputation due to poor working conditions and low salaries.

While this joint venture is new for the Olympics, private security companies have been active during many large-scale events internationally for decades. However, these companies have a short history in Japan. In the 1960s, the first Japanese PSC – the predecessor of today's SECOM – was founded and received positive feedback during the 1964 Olympics. At first, Japanese citizens were reluctant to acknowledge their role in society as crime rates were low and they believed security to be something taken for granted. When crime rates started to rise in the 1980s, a feeling of insecurity grew within Japanese society, and even after they began declining since 2004, feelings of insecurity remain. Media reporting as well as official crime statistics matter to the sense of security in Japanese society. Official police statistics change over time, also depending on which crimes are included or excluded from the statistics. Sensationalized media reporting on crime statistics often do not take these changes into account. PSCs obviously profit from high feelings of insecurity, as it is their job to provide security. The numbers support this assumption: Over the past 45 years the number of private security personnel increased from 41,146 in 1972 to 552,405 in 2017,[6] by far outnumbering the police at 296,702 in 2018.

During the Games, these security guards will mainly be responsible for onsite security. They will check the incoming visitors at the gates, install moving security centers, and aid in traffic control. Especially the last service is very common in Japan. In case of repair work on the streets or construction sites, PSC staff are a regular sight for controlling traffic and pedestrian flows. During the Olympics, Japanese PSCs emphasize that they will try their best to ensure that security checks will be conducted swiftly in order to prevent congestion at the gates. Facial recognition, about 2.5 times faster than barcode scanning, will be used to speed up the check-in time.

Surveillance as a legacy of Tokyo 2020?

How does Tokyo 2020 affect the city and what happens after the event? Even though security measures are generally accepted by the public to a certain degree, until recently there has been some resistance against the installment of security cameras in trains. Especially in its large urban centers, millions of Japanese commute daily by train, and many of the passengers take naps or surf the internet on their phones during their commutes. It was widely appreciated that – apart from a few trains – no cameras were in operation. However, crimes occurring on trains that received broad media coverage (such as a random knife attack on a Shinkansen bullet train in 2018) and the upcoming mega-event ultimately were used as sources of legitimation for tighter security measures. Once in operation, security cameras in trains or public spaces are not likely to be removed after the event. A large-scale advertising campaign by Tokyo Metro in 2019 tries to put a positive spin on camera surveillance in its stations and trains (see Figure 32.1). The tight cooperation between the police and the PSCs, once proven to be an effective method of crime prevention, will continue to be intensified. Just as during the Games in 1964, PSCs may once again receive positive feedback and will be assigned more tasks of social responsibility. 1964 was the opportunity to show that Japan is a country with advanced technology and back then, PSCs were still small in Japan. 2020, however, is the opportunity to present Japan as one of the world's safest countries. Although – or rather regardless of – a decreasing crime rate and increasing security awareness within Japanese society,

Figure 32.1 "Get strong, Tokyo", advertisement by Tokyo Metro.
Source: © Barbara Holthus.

security measures for the Olympic Games will not only provide security, but also permanently change the role and meaning of security in Japanese society.

Notes

1 Handelman, Don. 2016. "Prologue: Olympic surveillance as a prelude to securitization." In Bajc, Vida (ed.). *Surveilling and securing the Olympics*. London: Palgrave Macmillan: 5.
2 Bajc, Vida. 2016. "The Olympic Games as a complex planned event: Between uncertainty and order through security meta-ritual." In Bajc, Vida (ed.): *Surveilling and securing the Olympics*. London: Palgrave Macmillan: 24.
3 Ibid., 49.
4 Tagsold, Christian. 2016. "Modernity and the carnivalesque (Tokyo 1964)." In Bajc, Vida (ed.). *Surveilling and securing the Olympics*. London: Palgrave Macmillan: 107.
5 Abe, Kiyoshi. 2016. "Fear of the radical movements and policing the enemy within (Sapporo 1972)." In Bajc, Vida (ed.). *Surveilling and securing the Olympics*. London: Palgrave Macmillan: 141.
6 For 2017 data on PSCs in Japan, see www.npa.go.jp/safetylife/seianki/statistics/29keibi.pdf.

33 The Olympic and Paralympic Games as a technology showcase

Franz Waldenberger

With the world watching, the Olympic Games provide an ideal case to demonstrate national prowess, not only in the field of sports. When Japan hosted its 1964 Olympics, the Shinkansen, the world's first high-speed rail system, had just started operation. The 1964 Games were the first to be broadcasted via satellites and the first using electronic time measurement, a technology developed and deployed by the Japanese precision instrument company Seiko. These showcases of innovation and technological leadership demonstrated Japan's ambitions and potential, and within less than two decades, the country established itself as a leading high-tech nation.

Today, Japan is one of the most research-and-development intensive economies. The country tops international patent statistics and boasts one of the largest technology-trade surpluses. It was in Japan where the first mobile internet services were successfully launched in 1999. In 2013, the year Japan won the bid for the Olympics, the government officially declared to make Japan the world's most advanced IT nation. In 2016, this goal was topped by the vision to transform Japan into a "super smart" society and to lead the world into the next stage of human civilization, termed "Society 5.0."

Japan aims to use the Olympics to underline and showcase its ambitions as a frontrunner in the digital transformation. Tokyo 2020 is to be remembered as the "smart" Games. The 5G mobile communication network is to be deployed in time for the events to allow live-streaming and viewing systems using 3D and 360° technology. The national broadcasting company NHK plans to air events in ultra-high 8K resolution quality. Driverless vehicles will demonstrate Japan's advancements in the field of autonomous driving. At many locations, robots will provide spectators with information or serve refreshments. Japan also plans to digitally augment its world-renown hospitality with devices and applications offering automatic instantaneous translation. Surveillance technology including drones and state-of-the-art facial recognition software is to ensure the security and smooth operation of the Games.

There had also been news that the official fireworks at the opening and closing ceremonies might be replaced by man-made meteor showers, a technology developed by a Tokyo-based high-tech startup. However, that product will likely not be ready in time for the Games....

34 Tokyo 2020

Connecting the past with the future

Wolfram Manzenreiter in roundtable discussion with Munehiko Harada and John Horne

The following discussion between three Japan sport scholars is based on a DIJ Roundtable event, held October 20, 2018 at the German Institute for Japanese Studies in Tokyo.

WM = Wolfram Manzenreiter, Japanese studies, University of Vienna
JH = John Horne, sport sociology, Waseda University
MH = Munehiko Harada, sport management, Waseda University

WM: The Olympics have come a long way. It was French aristocrat Pierre de Coubertin in the 19th century who designed their organizational form and underlying principles of Olympism to cherish sportsmanship, mutual respect and peaceful unity of mankind at a time when Europe was suffering from the terror of war between modern nation-states.

JH: In the beginning, the International Olympic Committee was a compound fashioned out of various ideas about the pursuit of physical culture. Pierre de Coubertin was in particular taken with an English gentlemen's club in England that organized the Henley rowing regatta in Oxfordshire. In many ways the IOC remained essentially an elite club with many aristocrats among its members. But during the last decades, the Olympics have become a very well recognized global brand, turning it into a transnational enterprise.

WM: Early in the 20th century, the Olympics also were a composite of sport contests, art competitions, and exhibitions featuring tribal sports or national showcases.

JH: The early Olympic Games were held in conjunction with World Fairs. Since the transnational spread of color television, the Olympics have grown out of being nested within the international expositions. Currently these non-sport mega-events attract more visitors than the

Olympics – but hardly any media attention. The attraction of watching live sports makes the difference.

MH: From a marketing point of view, sport is a very special product, easy to buy, and easy to sell. It doesn't need much education or experience to understand what's going on in the competition. Everybody is a customer, no matter what race or class. When the Olympic Games started in 1896, they were like ketchup served on the side of the hamburger. But they grew and grew, with ups and downs like an elevator, and ultimately succeeded in the competition against other sport events trying to invade their property. This is kind of a survival of the fittest. Today the Olympic Rings are immediately recognized by 94% of all people. It's more than just a sports brand, representing friendship, excellence, and respect. Universal brand recognition like this is unique.

WM: Yet the Winter Olympics, which are riding on the same train using the same brand ticket, do not attract the same kind of global attention. They target a separate market of different customers.

JH: Winter Olympics, like the Paralympic Games, are smaller in terms of number of events, duration, participants, and broadcasts. Television reach and media coverage are growing, but only in some parts of the world. Basically, they are Games of the Global North. The recently established Youth Olympics equip the IOC with a third element to keep the brand alive. For similar reasons of maintaining brand awareness, the IOC decided on the alternating format of Summer and Winter Games. In the years in-between the IOC handpicks its favorite hosts from candidate cities.

Launching a bid

MH: Being a host city candidate is one thing, getting the bid another one. A successful candidate city must have everything first class. First class airport, first class hotels, first class transportation systems, first class economic situation. For the 2016 Games, a joint bid by Hiroshima and Nagasaki stepped into the ring with Tokyo. But the Japan Olympic Committee decided only Tokyo can do it.

JH: Britain similarly had bids coming forward from Birmingham and Manchester that ended in defeat. A newspaper article afterwards stated the only way Britain was going to get the Olympic Games was if London put itself forward. Only London has the world-class facilities the IOC is attracted to. Not many cities fit to their standards. If we were having this discussion in 2028, half of all Olympiads would still only have been officially assigned to six cities: London, Tokyo,

Los Angeles and Paris got the bid three times, Berlin and Athens twice. Launching a bid is not a cheap thing to do. Estimates I have seen for Tokyo run into multi-million dollars. We're talking here about campaigning managed by spin-doctors and companies with a proven track record in winning bids.

MH: Previously I helped Osaka bid for 2008. Before entering the bidding phase, we were very cautious about any contenders. So we asked China: "Are you coming for 2008?" They said: "No, we're not gonna do it.", "Are you sure?", "Yes we are sure." So we went for it. But right after that, China came and Beijing got the 2008 Games. Knowledge, experience, and relations are key. The JOC bid for 2016 failed but the insights gained during the process, and the human network we established, especially with IOC members, naturally secured the 2020 Games for Tokyo.

JH: Certainly persistence is needed. Pyeongchang kept going and made three consecutive bids before landing the 2018 Winter Olympics. Japan with the Osaka bid for 2008 has a history of persistence as well.

MH: People just told us don't quit, you have to keep bidding, you know, many times.

Narratives and message control

WM: It's the scarcity value of having the Olympic Rings that sustains bidding activities. Host cities aim for the unique situation to transmit powerful messages to the world.

JH: In 1964 Japan had its coming-out-party, showcasing modernity and technological development.

MH: In 1964 the message was very clear: recovery from World War II. The message from 2020 is different: how to maintain our infrastructure, particularly at times of rapid aging and population decline. Sydney 2000 became the Green Olympics, London 2012 were called the most connected, and Tokyo will be about artificial intelligence. We envision Tokyo 2020 as a showcase of how technologies deal with these problems.

What stays behind

WM: Inevitably it will take time to recoup expenses, if ever. Public finances in the red belong to the most frequent aftereffects of Olympic hosting. This is not the kind of legacies that the IOC has in mind when it encourages candidate cities to think ahead about what stays behind when submitting their bids.

JH: The IOC summarized 40 changes and recommendations in its "Agenda 20/20." It's got nothing to do with Tokyo 2020 specifically but deals with cost reduction, environmental protection, sustainability, and legacy building. Legacy has been around as a keyword in its association with mega-events for 20 years only. It is extremely popular as it holds at bay the concerns about gigantism, wastefulness, and the sustainability of something that critics would say is not sustainable. Legacy can cover what appears to be a kind of almost instantaneous change. But it can also mean something very long-term, which people are not going to see possibly in their lifetimes.

MH: We learned a lot from the London Games. They left a very good legacy, with the redevelopment of East London and the successful operating of many commercial areas. But the biggest legacy is tourism development. London did a wonderful campaign attracting millions of visitors to the UK. It hosted the Commonwealth Games in 2014, the Rugby World Cup in 2015 and other large athletic events, raising the number of annual visitors from 31 million in 2012 to 41 million most recently.

JH: Many cultural institutions in London however, such as the British Museum, reported their visitor numbers to be down by 25% to 30% during London 2012. I came across reports of the same displacement effects of regular tourists by sports tourists in 2000 in Sydney, disappointing many restaurants and business owners outside of the honeypot areas.

MH: Sports tourists spend about twice as much than average travelers. During the 2015 Rugby World Cup, their expenditure was even four times higher. If Japan manages to attract many sports tourists who spend more and stay longer, this would be a wonderful legacy for a shrinking society. With every Japanese we lose, consumption goes down by $12,000. Japan aims at welcoming 60 million inbound tourists per year.

For more information, photos, and the Podcast: www.dijtokyo.org/event/tokyo-2020-and-beyond-legacies-from-hosting-the-olympic-and-paralympic-summer-games/.

Index

For Product Safety Concerns and Information please contact our EU
representative GPSR@taylorandfrancis.com
Taylor & Francis Verlag GmbH, Kaufingerstraße 24, 80331 München, Germany

9 780367 471682